The Complete Guide
to Making
Environmentally Friendly
Investment Decisions

How to Make a Lot of Green Money
While Saving the Planet

Alan Northcott

THE COMPLETE GUIDE TO MAKING ENVIRONMENTALLY FRIENDLY INVESTMENT DECISIONS: HOW TO MAKE A LOT OF GREEN MONEY WHILE SAVING THE PLANET

Copyright © 2014 Atlantic Publishing Group, Inc.
1405 SW 6th Avenue • Ocala, Florida 34471 • Phone 800-814-1132 • Fax 352-622-1875
Website: www.atlantic-pub.com • E-mail: sales@atlantic-pub.com
SAN Number: 268-1250

Library of Congress Cataloging-in-Publication Data

Northcott, Alan, 1951-
  The complete guide to making environmentally friendly investment decisions : how to make a lot of green money while saving the planet / Alan Northcott.
     p. cm.
  Includes bibliographical references and index.
  ISBN-13: 978-1-60138-323-5 (alk. paper)
  ISBN-10: 1-60138-323-1 (alk. paper)
  1. Investments--Moral and ethical aspects. 2. Investments--Environmental aspects. 3. Environmentalism--Social aspects. 4. Social responsibility of business. I. Title.
  HG4515.13.N67 2011
  332.6--dc23
                        2011037466

Printed in the United States

INTERIOR LAYOUT: Antoinette D'Amore • addesign@videotron.ca
COVER DESIGN: Jackie Miller • sullmill@charter.net

14.49

Printed on Recycled Paper

332.6
Nor

A few years back we lost our beloved pet dog Bear, who was not only our best and dearest friend but also the "Vice President of Sunshine" here at Atlantic Publishing. He did not receive a salary but worked tirelessly 24 hours a day to please his parents.

Bear was a rescue dog who turned around and showered myself, my wife, Sherri, his grandparents Jean, Bob, and Nancy, and every person and animal he met (well, maybe not rabbits) with friendship and love. He made a lot of people smile every day.

We wanted you to know a portion of the profits of this book will be donated in Bear's memory to local animal shelters, parks, conservation organizations, and other individuals and nonprofit organizations in need of assistance.

– *Douglas & Sherri Brown*

PS: We have since adopted two more rescue dogs: first Scout, and the following year, Ginger. They were both mixed golden retrievers who needed a home.

Want to help animals and the world? Here are a dozen easy suggestions you and your family can implement today:

- *Adopt and rescue a pet from a local shelter.*
- *Support local and no-kill animal shelters.*
- *Plant a tree to honor someone you love.*
- *Be a developer — put up some birdhouses.*
- *Buy live, potted Christmas trees and replant them.*
- *Make sure you spend time with your animals each day.*
- *Save natural resources by recycling and buying recycled products.*
- *Drink tap water, or filter your own water at home.*
- *Whenever possible, limit your use of or do not use pesticides.*
- *If you eat seafood, make sustainable choices.*
- *Support your local farmers market.*
- *Get outside. Visit a park, volunteer, walk your dog, or ride your bike.*

Five years ago, Atlantic Publishing signed the Green Press Initiative. These guidelines promote environmentally friendly practices, such as using recycled stock and vegetable-based inks, avoiding waste, choosing energy-efficient resources, and promoting a no-pulping policy. We now use 100-percent recycled stock on all our books. The results: in one year, switching to post-consumer recycled stock saved 24 mature trees, 5,000 gallons of water, the equivalent of the total energy used for one home in a year, and the equivalent of the greenhouse gases from one car driven for a year.

Dedication

Dedicated to my beautiful wife, Liz, my constant companion through life's adventures and strength for more than 30 years.

Table of Contents

Chapter 4: Solar Power 79

Chapter 5: Wind and Wave Power 95

Introduction

The evidence is all around. Climate change is no longer just a theory; it has an increasing impact on all parts of the world. There are still a few who deny its reality, generally by referring to its earlier name of "global warming" and pointing to extreme cold conditions in certain areas of the world, but the scientific evidence is overwhelming.

The world is awakening to the possibility of a massive and irretrievable crisis that many would blame on the environmental impact of our modern lifestyle. Climate change is accepted by the majority of people, and most think it is caused by the profligate lifestyle we have developed. In 1988, Lance Morrow writing in *Time* magazine said the U.S. had "a talent for somehow outdistancing problems in a headlong race toward something new." Sadly, it seems that events are catching up, and running can no longer allow us to outpace the truth.

The matter of a social conscience in investing has been discussed for decades. Although not always concerned with environmental matters, socially conscious investing in worthy products and businesses and avoiding those that were thought to be harmful, whether tobacco, the defense industry, or some other pariah, sometimes has required self-sacrifice to the extent of accepting lower portfolio returns and eschewing high earners.

For instance, weapons companies may be a part of a profitable industry when the United States is involved in two major wars, but the socially responsible investor may choose to eschew such choices in adhering to his or her standards. Although many people still think that socially responsible investing is a worthy concept, when it comes to their personal financial portfolios and saving for retirement, they may have cause to consider how much investing in such companies would cost them personally in lost potential returns.

The current movement, which goes under various names such as green investing, clean investing, envirotech, and cleantech, does not necessarily need the sacrifices socially responsible investing requires. This situation is changing as grants and subsidies are helping consumers make more environmentally friendly choices, and companies in this field are becoming larger and more competitive. Greentech is becoming a hot topic and is generating a lot of interest in both existing companies and startups. The necessity for this transformation to happen sooner rather than later to deal with the crises the world is facing means there will be vast profits to be made in developing environmentally friendly processes and equipment.

In this book, you will find details of the current state of the various industries involved in this movement and learn about some of the technologies in which you can invest. Some are still in the embryonic stage, while others have progressed to prototypical and production levels. Whatever you are considering investing in, you need to develop an understanding of the applied technologies that are involved to make a rational decision, as well as be aware of the potential pitfalls. Environmentally friendly products will be an increasing part of our lives over the next few decades, and there will be many opportunities to profit from this expansion.

When first approaching the topic of green investing, it may seem limited to some obvious categories, such as solar power, hybrid cars, and other popular ideas. When you delve deeper, however, you can see how most of the choices that you make in life involve some element of impact on the environment and by definition probably can be made greener. It is not possible to do anything without consequences and results, and it behooves us all as custodians of the planet to pay attention to our personal habits. At the end of the investing discussion, we look at ways our own lives may be framed to reduce our personal contributions to the problem.

In this way, it is more important than ever to invest in and encourage greentech research and manufacture. Money expands the development of less environmentally harmful products, no matter the industry, cannot simultaneously be helping maintain existing sometime polluting alternatives, so the very act of deciding to purposefully invest in green technologies is a powerful statement and influence on improving the environment.

Inevitably, this book is a snapshot in time looking at the current state of industry in 2014. If you are smitten by the technologies discussed here and wish to stay ahead of the curve, you would be well advised to consider subscribing to magazines that reveal the research and developments on the horizon. The mainstream science and technical journals highlight in layman's terms the areas seeing breakthroughs. Although the reporting is often about innovations that are far from marketable, it will allow you to become cognizant of the possibilities so when a future investment opportunity arises, you already will be familiar with the science and the potential issues that can arise.

It is important to recognize that where there is a great deal of research and innovation, there are also many failed ideas, so to invest wholeheartedly in any green technology would be foolish. As the concepts develop, there will be winners and losers, and the green market will be more volatile than established industries for some time. With that said, some established industries stand to suffer as new concepts are developed and as public feeling against "dirty" processes becomes stronger, so it may not be possible to achieve the same profits by staying invested in the older industries.

We both individually and as a society need to respond to our planet's cries of pain and take steps to minimize future harm. However, there is little doubt that we already have inflicted dramatic changes, the consequences of which may not yet be fully realized. Although this will affect the way everyone in this world must live in the coming decades, it also can represent unprecedented opportunities for innovation and novel thinking, which will give knowledgeable and involved investors several opportunities for profit.

The intention of this book is to provide the knowledge we presently have, discuss the different technologies being established to help combat the consequences of our previous actions and develop future sustainable lifestyles. There are many different approaches that may make sense in this context and, consequently, many investment opportunities.

Throughout the book, you will find sections detailing case studies of people involved in cleantech in some way. The first one is from Rona Fried, who is involved in news and networking and publishes a monthly newsletter called *Progressive Investor*.

CASE STUDY: KEEPING UP-TO-DATE

Rona Fried, Ph.D.
President and founder
SustainableBusiness.com
rona@sustainablebusiness.com

Rona Fried, Ph.D. is president and founder of SustainableBusiness.com, a global news and networking website dedicated to green business. Online since 1996, it was one of the first in the world to focus on green business, green jobs, and green investing.

Known as a thought leader in the field, SustainableBusiness.com provides daily green business and daily green investor news that cuts across all relevant sectors including renewable energy, energy efficiency, green building, smart grid, water, and the organic industry.

One of its services is Progressive Investor, *an online monthly newsletter that guides investors toward creating a green portfolio. It covers trends and companies worldwide in all the above sectors. Dr. Fried selects the stocks for the family of NASDAQ Green Economy Indexes and serves on the advisory board of three clean energy indexes. She is widely quoted as an expert in green business and green investing.*

When we first began publishing *Progressive Investor* in 2002, there were only a couple dozen "green" publicly traded companies — now there are more than 600 worldwide. That is just an example of how much the field of green business has exploded over the past decade. We launched the newsletter to help investors understand the criteria in choosing green companies and to help them develop green portfolios. It was part of our overall mission of helping green businesses grow by demonstrating their value to the economy and to investor profits.

The most rewarding aspect of doing this work has been observing and participating in the growth of green business in all its various forms. Seeing sectors such as solar, wind, and natural foods grow from tiny, marginal industries to mainstream powerhouses and common names has been very exciting. Watching new technologies emerge and capture the imagination of investors, driving their value higher, has been exhilarating.

Take First Solar, for example, which formed in 1999 and went public in late 2006. When pundits said thin-film solar would go nowhere, the company proved them wrong. It brought a new solar technology into the mainstream while drastically increasing solar efficiency and reducing the costs. Today, the company is a solar powerhouse with gigawatts of manufacturing capacity.

Then there is Chipotle Mexican Grill, a chain of more than 1,000 restaurants in the U.S., which is showing the fast food industry that it can source from organic farms. It serves 100 percent free-range chicken and pork, 85 percent beef, rBGH-free dairy products, organic produce, and beans. The goal is to offer a completely sustainable menu as soon as they can build the supply chain to meet their demand.

And we have seen the emergence of entirely new industries in energy storage, smart grid, LED lighting, and clean transportation.

Every sector of green business, such as renewable energy, efficiency, green building, and organic food production, has gone through the same trajectory. Each has fought against the forces of the status quo — the fossil fuel industry, the conventional real estate industry, and traditional agriculture — which, for decades promulgated that these new industries produced products that cost too much and did not perform well. Slowly, but surely, they have proven themselves and, in fact, are growing at much higher rates than their conventional counterparts.

This has been the hardest part of being in green business. We know that our products improve performance and actually lower costs over the long run, and they are crucial for the quality of life of the billions of people who occupy this planet (and the millions of other species).

And this is what drives my work — showing people they can invest in companies that make the world a better place, rather than those that may offer short-term profits at the expense of our planet's ecosystems and its people's health and welfare.

For eight years, we produced the SB20 — The World's Top Sustainable Companies. A group of judges, portfolio managers at leading green mutual funds and ETFs, selected the 20 companies. The purpose was to showcase the most innovative, model companies that, through their products or initiatives, are contributing substantially to the advance of a sustainable economy. We carefully chose a mix of companies representing all sizes, from regions across the world and across industries. Some of the outstanding companies that graced the list over the years include: IBM (IBM), Google (GOOG), Chipotle Mexican Grill (CMG), First Solar (FSLR), Herman Miller (MLHR), Philips Electronics (PHG), Timberland (TBL), and Interface (IFSIA).

The biggest challenge has been hanging in there throughout it all. For example, I never expected it would take this long to address climate change and that it would become such a partisan issue. I never could have anticipated the fossil fuel industry could convince the entire Republican Party that climate change is a hoax and to turn against science completely when scientific consensus is that climate change is fast approaching an irreversible tipping point. The Arctic ice was the smallest on record this year, we are experiencing the wettest, stormiest years on record with massive floods in Pakistan and Australia, but humanity still has yet to connect the dots.

So, while I focus on green investing, what is behind it is my urgent desire for the world to wake up and do what is best for itself … there is not much time left.

Chapter 1

Green Is the New Gold

In some ways, it is misleading to talk about green investing. Green investing can mean many different things, just as clean technology covers most of our current actions in living in this world. Whether it is developing a cleaner automobile, for which there are various options, replacing automobiles with more public transportation, ensuring our home heating and cooling is more efficient and less polluting, or any other myriad things that we do each day, there is usually some environmental impact and some aspect that can be made cleaner. The term green investing therefore can be applied to the whole range of products and manufacturing processes, and to some extent most businesses will have to adapt and become greener, if not voluntarily, then by government action.

Energy

One of the industries that has the most impact on our climate is the energy sector. The types and sources of energy that we typically use every day may not be ones that can be supported in the future in a greener world, particularly when it comes to transportation. There are many choices to make regarding how electricity is produced to power homes, offices, and other buildings. With the established nature and pervasiveness of electric power use, it is unlikely that there will be any swing against using electricity in principle, and generally, it is "clean" at the point of use, with no intrinsic pollution.

The building industry has embraced the need for building efficiency and has developed various standards related to ongoing energy usage and energy used to create the building in the first place. These standards are embodied in the Leadership in Energy and Environmental Design (LEED) standard in the United States. Internationally, other countries are further advanced than the United States, due in part to the Kyoto Protocol that was adopted in late 1997 and came into force in 2005. This protocol requires participating countries to reduce their emissions by set amounts. The U.S. has never agreed to this; most U.S. officials argue that it would hurt business.

Energy as a green topic has several angles, including the way energy is generated and its effective use. Some energy savings can be made by various means, such as with insulation and building orientation in the case of building heating and cooling, but there is also the field of effective energy usage as typified by the "smart grid." *This will be discussed in Chapter 6.*

Because all industries need some sort of power to operate, what happens in the energy industry has a direct effect on how clean a company's operations can become. With that said, there are many processes that create pollution or emit unwanted vapors, and technology that tackles these may be worthwhile investments. *The opportunities for green investing are extensive and are broken down in later chapters.*

Water

In the past, water has been considered freely or cheaply available. That is not going to be the case in the future. Some countries always have found it difficult to provide clean water for their inhabitants' basic needs, and others already are finding it increasingly problematic to maintain adequate supplies.

At first sight from space, one might wonder how anyone on Earth could have a problem getting enough water. Two-thirds of the Earth is covered in oceans and seas, and even away from these areas, there are lakes and rivers and the prospect of digging wells. Some countries — the less naturally hospitable ones and poorer ones such as parts of Africa — always have faced problems with providing water for their increasing populations, but the complications are set to spread more widely. The U.S.'s comparative wealth largely has prevented any issues from arising to date, but despite this, the current North American systems already are reaching a breaking point. In this century, Colorado water, which is routinely transported to serve several Western desert states, has been in short supply with some nearby desert towns nearly reaching the brink of disaster.

Of course, the vast quantities of water in the oceans are not suitable for drinking or for crop irrigation without treatment, and desalination plants are just one of the opportunities for investors in the future. Profligate use of a seeming unending supply in the past has had its detrimental effects, and it is only now that research has turned to ways of using water more efficiently and recycling effectively in industrialized nations. *Water will be discussed further in Chapter 8.* For now, it is sufficient to note that the current global market for usable water is valued at nearly half a trillion dollars annually, third only to electricity and oil in terms of market size.

Carbon Trading

Thanks to the perceived need to do something about the environmental factors of our daily lives, we now have a burgeoning interest in our "carbon footprint" and in the amount of carbon generated into the atmosphere. It is fashionable to be able to boast that our lives or a company's operations are "carbon neutral." This is more a topic of conversation in other parts of the world than in the U.S. due to both government and individual attitudes in recent years, but the average American citizen is becoming increasingly aware of the concept of carbon neutrality, and in due time, this awareness will spread throughout the world.

All this interest in the carbon cost of activity has resulted in various trading methods to offset the sometimes-inevitable carbon production, and the concept of carbon trading has formed as a result. Essentially, it allows a carbon polluter to offset his or her carbon production by making payments to someone who has a negative polluting effect — in the simplest form, perhaps someone who plants forests that help absorb carbon dioxide from the air.

There are not many ways in which this negative effect can be realized, but the system of carbon trading allows a certain amount of pollution from various processes, and industries can buy and sell this allowance. If a company does not use all of its "carbon credits," it can sell the excess to a company that needs them. Thus, the company makes a profit from this in addition to its main source of business. A new trading market has formed to facilitate these deals. Once again, Europe leads the way in this, as the concept was spawned from the Kyoto Protocol that the United States has not adopted. But America is catching up quickly by establishing a global carbon market called the Green Exchange, sometimes shortened to GreenX. *Carbon and other emissions can be traded in several ways. These are discussed in Chapter 12.*

Agriculture

In 2014, even in the United States where the consumer generally is cushioned from the worst problems of the world, the price of food has risen significantly. There are a number of reasons for this, not the least of which is that the world population has risen to 7 billion with a projected rise to more than 8 billion by 2020. Currently, more than 1 billion people in the world are considered undernourished. Eighty percent of U.S. ethanol is produced from corn. Biofuel is currently subsidized, with the ethanol industry receiving about $6 billion in subsidies, arguably no longer necessary; Australia, where the world obtains a large amount of its wheat, was recently suffering from extensive flooding; and Argentina, which is the world's top exporter of soybeans, suffered from a drought. Many still argue whether these factors are directly related to climate change, but the fact is that the world's agricultural resources are already stretched, and increasing food prices is the inevitable consequence.

In the long-term view, the amount of water available from rivers, lakes, and aquifers is diminishing, and the alternative of desalinated seawater is more expensive, which inevitably will increase the cost of agricultural production. Present farming methods are not the most ecologically beneficial practices and lay the land open to erosion. Forcibly cropping the most profitable plants instead of using plant rotation to restore the soil naturally requires adding more chemicals and nutrients, which adds to the cost and makes the crops more open to disease. When you factor in the decline in fish populations around the world, it is plain to see that a food crisis is looming.

Although at this stage it might be difficult to identify just how the agricultural issues will be resolved, whenever there is a crisis, there will be an opportunity for investment and profit. At one stage, it was believed that genetically modified (GM) plants could hold the secret to improving food production, but significant issues surround using genetic modification, and not all parties are at ease. It is not as simple as investing in Monsanto (a company that has already captured much of the GM market and helps farmers use fewer resources to produce more food) and waiting for the profits to roll in. There inevitably will be some ups and downs when using GM, as the increasing popularity of organic food, despite its generally higher cost, shows. *The looming agricultural crisis is discussed in more detail in Chapter 11.*

Pollution

It is difficult to be aware environmentally without soon facing the reality of pollution. Up until this point in history, energy, water, land, and natural resources had seemed to be so abundant that there was little need to be concerned about throwing away old products and packaging when they had served their useful purpose. But in a more ecologically minded world, there is no excuse for packaging that is more than necessary for simple protection and identification of the product or for throwing away products and replacing them as soon as there is a problem rather than trying to repair them.

Nonetheless, for some time there will be an ample supply of waste because new developments have not been focused on eliminating our throwaway society, and it is doubtful that waste can ever be eliminated completely. This raises the question of how best to dispose of waste in a way other than putting it in landfills and allowing its gradual decomposition, which releases methane gases into the atmosphere. One of the solutions that has been implemented is burning trash to generate electricity. This seems to be a good use, because otherwise unusable material now produces energy, but it is not something that can be considered a green process. Even with emissions rules, the typical incinerator will still release unacceptable amounts of carbon dioxide into the atmosphere, similar to those from conventional coal plants, not to mention the various chemicals that come from the materials burning.

Alternatives to incineration are being developed, although it is difficult now to see which may be the winning technologies. It is obvious we must find alternatives to domestic waste disposal, just as we must find alternatives to industrial pollution by developing different or modified processes. The finite nature of the earth and the continually expanding amount of pollution if there is no change in our practices are irreconcilable, and there will be cash in trash for the winning technologies and their investors. *Pollution is discussed in more depth in Chapter 12.*

The Opportunities

Some of the options mentioned above have been floating around in the public consciousness for many years, so you may wonder why making environmentally friendly investment decisions are any more appropriate or profitable today than in previous years. After all, for decades, some people have been advocating socially conscious investing, and it has not always been considered to be as profitable as investing in businesses that pay no attention to being socially conscious and are even wasteful and polluting.

Those who have a long enough memory may recall the drama of the late 1970s. During President Jimmy Carter's administration, oil prices soared to new heights, and there was a rush to fund research into **coal gasification** (one of the cleanest ways to convert coal into electricity), extracting oil from shale, and other measures. But this was a reaction to an artificially created shortage caused possibly by Saudi Arabia limiting exports. When the politics were resolved, there was still a good supply of oil in the ground, the prices receded, and research abated. Nowadays, the situation is different with oil fields in decline and the phrase **peak oil** (which means the peak rate of oil production has been passed) being bandied about. Peak oil rises every year, and it is difficult to know if peak oil has occurred, as many suppliers are reticent to reveal their true reserves and available rate of production (if indeed they know them), but many other industry observers feel the first decade of the new century may have seen peak oil slip by.

A decade ago, the tech bubble also aroused a lot of interest in alternative energy when it seemed that science and technology could just keep powering the economy by breaking down more conventional barriers. Unfortunately, this bubble burst, and technical stocks plunged, headed by failure of the dot-com boom. Just ten years later, we have important signs that the current interest in green energy and clean technology may not disappear like a passing fad. With steady developmental progress, green energy is nearing commercial viability in many areas and may only be a few years away in others. Once this is recognized as a viable energy option, there will be no constraints to expanding the demand, and the emphasis will swing over to supply and keeping up with the needs.

Green investments are becoming mainstream, with major investment banks and mutual funds starting to put money into various technologies such as wind and solar power. Alternatively, it increasingly is becoming recognized that the technologies we currently use are contributing to a potentially disastrous scenario of increasing climate change, the extent of which, even if all emissions ceased immediately, is still unknown.

On the energy front, although science has developed the sophistication to continue satisfying a seemingly insatiable demand, shale oil and oil drilling technologies that allow horizontal drilling (literally a way for drilling to progress horizontally underground to increase the area that can be accessed from one location) and the consequential extraction from large areas can only serve to delay the inevitable — the recognition that oil supplies are unable to keep up with modern demands. Instead of releasing the populace from the demands of commuting to work as was earlier promised, the Internet has only made us more power hungry, and the amount of telecommuting has not scratched at the problem. New electronic devices are increasing the power needs of the typical consumer, and U.S. electrical demand is predicted to rise dramatically to keep up.

Even this only considers the domestic front. With increasing wealth in developing countries, world energy consumption will increase greatly. The Chinese and Indians see the Western way of life as something to aspire to. They are rapidly increasing their needs and are requiring many more motorcars and gadgets each year to fuel the catch-up process.

All this may lead you to wonder why you need to study green investing at all and why you do not simply move your portfolio into the stocks of those companies that are developing green technologies. The truth is that it is a dangerous time to be investing in markets that are in different stages of gestation. As with all investing, it is necessary to be prudent and research the different opportunities to determine which are most likely to create profit and to succeed in the end. There are various opportunities, and not all will succeed. In fact, if you compare green investing to the recent bubble in Internet stocks, you will see that many companies fail when an industry is in its infancy, even though the potential means that a few will profit greatly. Another reason to be cautious is that green investing covers many different technologies and markets, as you can see from the small selection listed above. Each one of the technologies faces different challenges in coming to market, and to treat the investment as a homogenous whole is asking for trouble. In the simplest of examples, solar power and wind power are both viable, though perhaps uneconomical without the subsidies that are currently available. They also can be presented in different ways, from residential installations to vast electricity farms, each with their constraints and rewards. In some circumstances, these two technologies may turn out to be competitors, with the success of one spelling the end of the other, or they may be used in a complementary fashion.

Some of the green technologies already work, some are in active production, and some are just concepts at the moment. Apart from specific technology companies, it is important to remember other facets of the equation, such as producers of the raw materials used in these technologies, as these surely will benefit from green successes. In considering where to invest, you must be careful to take a global perspective — the technology is advancing more rapidly in other countries in many cases where their needs have dictated. For instance, Europe has much stricter environmental legislation, and consequently, the public is more accepting of the idea of a carbon footprint there. This means that some of the major companies in wind and solar power are not U.S.-based at present. Although the U.S. no doubt will endeavor to catch up, if you are looking for immediate investment opportunities, include foreign companies in your assessment.

The Naysayers

Now, there is a certain section of society that would suggest investors are better off putting their money in the computing and engineering sectors on the basis that they will profit from solving all our environmental problems. After all, for decades, our technological society has been meeting problems head-on and providing innovative engineering solutions. Such an attitude denies the basic laws of physics. Engineering and invention only can take us to a certain point. If raw materials such as oil are in short supply, if the climate and our health are threatened by toxic emissions, science can only do so much to mitigate those problems. Our lives are in constant repair, and each year we face new challenges to undo the results of the previous year's crisis. It is easy to be in denial and blame the companies, the government, the unions, and anyone else involved, but at the end of the day, society makes the demands that cause the problems. The purpose of this book is to point you in the direction of green investments, but it is worth considering *why* there needs to be a change in attitude this time.

Society's journey toward self-destruction has been well documented in previous environmental reports and will only be recounted here in summary form. The Greek philosophers captured the essence of life and recognized that the world had within it the seeds of decay. In Greek mythology, history is presented in five stages, each of which is more degraded and harsher than the previous one. The first, the Golden Age, was considered the most abundant and happiest, with the successive ages of Silver, Brass, Heroic, and Iron being progressively more difficult. The idea of time decaying society was central to Greek philosophy. Both Plato and Aristotle believed that the best social order was the one that changed the world the least. They believed growth did not create greater value and order, but rather the opposite. The goal of the intellectual Greek was to pass on to the next generation a world as little changed as possible.

Moving on to the post-Christ era, the medieval view was that life was a resting place to prepare for the next world. Christian theology recognizes life as a decaying process, an inexorable journey, with life controlled by God and good or bad events being God's will. The idea of original sin precluded the possibility of improving your position. The son of the village blacksmith would desire to be the next village blacksmith, rather than aspiring to what we would now consider "greater things." Once again, personal growth and gain had nothing to do with life's purpose.

It seems our modern societal attitudes and self-destructive tendencies had their foundation with Sir Francis Bacon who, in his *Novum Organum* published in 1620, advocated the scientific method for seeking objective knowledge. He was followed by mathematician René Descartes, who sought to measure and reduce nature to mere algebra, and by Sir Isaac Newton, whose three laws of motion defined nature as a mechanical world. Shunning the idea of maintaining the status quo and opening the vision of continuous "improvement," tacitly defined as exploring and exploiting as much as possible in the name of science, these pioneers instigated a sea change or transformation in world vision. This transformation has been so complete that it seems almost impossible to entertain the idea that "progress" can be anything other than desirable and the purpose of man's endeavors.

Meanwhile, on the economic front, Adam Smith did for the economy what Newton had done for physics, and as a result, the largely unspoken belief that by reducing the society to mere mechanics we ultimately could control it meant modern society's decline was cemented in our collective consciousness. "Progress" is now, without doubt, the goal of our lives, and such progress is measured in curious ways, of which there many examples, including for instance maximizing crop yields per acre of land with no account for the cost and pollution of the chemicals used to achieve them.

Several hundred years of history have set the world's course and the profligacy with which we carelessly squander resources. Some say there will need to be a paradigm shift before we truly can understand what lies in the future, and it is best to bear this in mind when determining those technologies that actually will benefit and expand in coming decades. Once again, not all of the answers will be present investment options, and investment options will develop at different rates, but if you can keep in mind the direction society must take rather than relying on what has proved to work in the past, you will be better placed to assess the safe harbors and opportunities for your investments.

Industry Readiness

Having established that there is a need for clean technology development in the coming years, how can we determine that some technologies are at least at a stage where they are worthy of investment? To decide this, look at the history of some of the technologies being brought to market. Here are some examples of promising industries that are only growing in popularity with investors.

Solar photovoltaic power

Despite its apparent novelty on the market given the degree of popularity it has received thus far, the technology behind the solar photovoltaic power that directly generates electricity has been known for more than 50 years. Electricity was first generated from sunlight in the Bell Laboratories in 1954. The fundamental principles were discovered much earlier than this first experimentation into practical application.

Wind power

Wind power, though barely producing much more electricity than solar power, has an even longer history to draw on, even though early windmills were not directed toward electricity production but merely mechanical work, such as the grinding of flour or the pumping of water.

Fuel-efficient vehicles

Currently, hybrid and electric vehicles are in commercial production. Hydrogen fuel cells were thought to be a viable option a few years ago, but they currently are lacking practical large-scale development due in part to the fact that there has been little done to create a network of hydrogen delivery around the country to refuel them, a "chicken-and-egg" situation. Another environmentally sound option for those wishing to invest in the green automotive industry is biofuels. Ethanol

from corn is just one biofuel option, and it is one investment option that has reached commercial markets, even if it is somewhat flawed in concept because of the competition between ethanol and food needs.

Construction and building resource usage

As you will see in Chapter 9 on green buildings, the construction industry is finally bringing sustainability and green principles in building and operation to fruition after many years of paying lip service. During the twentieth century, it became the practice to create larger buildings and homes to impress, and those who lived through that time will well remember the "thermal shock" on entering upmarket resorts and shops, where the air conditioning was so cold you felt like putting on more clothes when you went inside. Fortunately, attitudes are changing, and it is now considered reasonable to build with more care to match the needs of the occupants.

Thus, there are many choices for clean and green investing in the marketplace, with others to be developed commercially in the near future. Now is the ideal time to take an interest in what will be the boom industries in coming decades.

Chapter 2

Investing Guidelines

This book will introduce you to many different clean-tech and green technologies, and as such, enable you to be better informed when you are exploring possible investments. There is nothing worse than an investor who makes choices based on other people's recommendations without exercising due diligence and then complains if the investment does not perform as anticipated. Armed with the knowledge in this book, you should be capable of making your own evaluations.

It is assumed that you are looking for medium to long-term investments and not trading frequently. Short-term trading is a way potentially to make a profit out of the markets quickly and is based mainly on technical analysis, which is a method to assess and try to exploit the mood or sympathy of the traders in the market. As such, it is not necessarily related to the underlying value of the investment but merely how it is perceived at any particular time. In the longer term, fundamental analysis aims to identify companies and shares with the possibility of real value growth, rather than exploiting short-term fluctuations.

The investor should be familiar with general accounting procedures and company reports, as regardless of the industry being researched the company must stand on its merits in accordance with usual business practices. However high-tech, whiz-bang, or green the products are, unless the company is being run in an efficient way, it is not a place for your investment. As a reminder, here are some of the fundamentals you should take into account when looking into any company's affairs.

Fundamental Investing

The fundamental investor believes that a well-run company on the path to increased profits will be a sound place to invest in, and the shares will increase in value. The Efficient Market Hypothesis, first proposed by Fama in the 1960s, avers that share values are based on all available information at any time, thus, no advantage can gained by buying and selling. Traders and investors buy shares in the hope that they are worth more than the price paid and sell shares they think are worth less than the selling price, but with efficient markets no one can know this, and the stock market comes down to a game of chance with random price fluctuations.

Although the Efficient Market Hypothesis has advocates and detractors, there is general agreement that, even if not correctly priced at a particular time, the general trend of a stock price will tend to reflect the true company value in due course. The value of the company can be determined by analyzing all the known information about the company, such as sales figures, profit margins, value of plant and equipment, economic outlook, etc.

The fundamental investor must be prepared to ride out the daily and weekly fluctuations in stock prices that come from many causes, such as news items, blogs, and rumors affecting traders' sentiments and, hence, share prices. Companies that are in the clean-tech and green business fields are particularly prone to this, as the latest research and development can impact perceptions if not the values markedly.

Some analysts prefer to divide stocks into different classes, such as growth stocks and value stocks. The theory is that growth stocks are those where the chief emphasis is on earnings growth, and value stocks are those that seem to be bargains, with an apparently cheap price for the value you will receive. Some investors also identify income stocks, which are generally those stocks that pay regular dividends and thus provide income, and momentum stocks that are generally rapidly growing companies, such as in emerging technologies. Regardless of classification, you should review each company in terms of how it meets your investment goals, including risk and potential return. Some stocks qualify under more than one classification, so these are only general guidelines.

The fundamental driver of share prices is the income or capital growth the company can achieve. Shares are only worth what can be realized out of holding them, and there are many other investments competing for the funds. If the shares pay a dividend, it is an easy task to value them, as the percentage dividends paid per year can be compared to investing in savings accounts or in bonds. Even then, some estimate of capital growth may need to be figured into the equation.

P/E ratio

One common measure of a company's value is the price/earnings (P/E) ratio. If a stock costs $50, and the earnings per share (EPS), that is, the total earnings per year divided by the number of shares issued by the company, is $5, the P/E is 50/5, or 10. Roughly speaking, this would equate to a 10-percent return on the investment, but this would depend on the amount the company chose to issue in dividends and how much it reinvested in plant and research.

When you are reviewing even such a simple ratio as the P/E, it is important to compare like with like. Sometimes the earnings are projected, sometimes they are based on the previous year, and sometimes they combine forward projection with past earnings. You are likely to come across these differences particularly when looking at younger companies in which projections may be the best information that they have. The P/E ratio usually is viewed and compared with other companies in the same industry sector in order to determine how well the subject company is performing. Different industries tend to have different "normal" P/Es, for example the banking industry numbers are usually fairly low, up to about 12, and yet high-tech companies have had P/Es up to the triple digits. Perhaps inevitably, these usually were not sustained and occurred most commonly before a crash.

If the company you are interested in has a P/E of 12, and other companies in the same industry average a P/E of 15, it appears the company is trading at a discount, in this case 80 percent of the typical company. Although on the face of it it should, this is by no means a guarantee that the company is better value, and you need to use caution before taking this as the go-ahead for an investment. There may be other reasons why the P/E is lower than competing companies; so exercise due diligence in determining if this is the case. Although some investors place a lot of store in a P/E ratio, it is worth noting that William J. O'Neil, who founded the *Investors Business Daily*, felt that the stock P/E ratio was less important than the company's earnings and the annual rate of increase in the earnings.

P/S ratio

Another ratio used by investors is called the price/sales ratio, or P/S. Some investors maintain that the P/S is a better indicator of share value than the

P/E. The sales figures are again divided by the total number of shares issued by the company in calculating this ratio, and the advantage/disadvantage, depending on your point of view, of this form is that it does not take into account expenses and debt. The greatest advantage is probably that sales figures are more difficult to manipulate than earnings, so this ratio gives a truer picture of the company's financial position.

Different experts feel several other ratios are indicative of a company's economic health. It can be important to compare the company's book value to its market price. In this case the book value is what the firm's accountants have decided the company is worth as calculated in accordance with standard procedures, commonly by subtracting the company's debts from the company's asset value — though there are some variations on this formula. The market price is the number of shares outstanding multiplied by the price per share, in fact just a measure of what investors sense the company is worth. These figures usually are combined to give the price-to-book ratio (P/B), which also can be known as the price/equity ratio. If this ratio is low, it can mean that the stock is undervalued or trading at a discount or other issues that may apply. If the ratio is high, you should be wary, and if you are paying more than two times the book value, you are probably spending too much.

Debt

Investors look at other figures to do with the company's value. Some companies trade with a modest amount of equity and borrow the money they need to operate. The higher the amount of borrowing, the more difficult it is for the company to service the debt and make a profit and the more vulnerable it is to interest rate changes. The debt ratio is the amount of debt the company holds in comparison to the stock market price, the number of shares times the price per share. If the debt is as much as 50 percent of the share investor's stake, the company is susceptible to changes in the lending market. No debt is ideal, but 25 percent may be a typical operating figure. As for the other ratios, the best way to determine if a particular company you are researching has a problem is to compare it with other companies in the same industry and sector, as these ratios vary in different markets.

Some investors like to explore how much institutional ownership there is in a company. The theory behind this practice is that institutional investors have access to extensive research and, therefore, should be better armed to make sound investment decisions. In fact, institutions account for more than 70 percent of trading volume. As with the other indicators, this is useful information but should be viewed in the context of the company you are looking at. Certainly, there are restrictions on where institutional funds usually are placed, and some fund managers have too much money to be able to invest in companies in the startup stage. Just because the largest institutions are not investing in a company does not mean you should ignore it, but you need to assess whether there are viable reasons for the company being disregarded.

Beta

Of the generally considered factors, it is worth looking at the beta of a company. The beta simply compares the volatility of a stock price to the general market. If the beta is 1.0, that means the stock price should move up and down as the market does. If the beta is 2.0, the stock price is likely to move twice as quickly as the market, which may give the potential investor a wild ride. A beta of less than one is less volatile, and a zero value implies the stock price is not influenced by what happens to the market at all. It is even possible to have negative beta values, and this would mean the price tends to move in the opposite direction of the general market. This is certainly a value to consider when reflecting on your propensity for risk.

Balancing your investments

Balancing your investments is an important exercise you must undertake in the light of your goals for the money and your time horizons. Many portfolios are assembled to maximize returns, often in a tax-advantaged account, to provide for retirement living. Some portfolios may have a different purpose, for example, to grow an account to provide for college funds for a newborn, and each must be treated differently. On top of this, some investors are more prepared to let the market's ups and downs happen without worrying, and others may be concerned if the portfolio loses more than a few percent.

It is not the purpose of this book to cover these topics, which are explained in detail in other reference books, but it is right to point out that, for instance, you usually will not have all your funds exposed to the volatility of shares, but include some fixed return bonds or money market accounts. Although the focus of this book is on companies and shares that can be called "green," this does not mean you should ignore these other types of investments that you must include where applicable for your investment profile.

Even after you have set up your portfolio and are happy with the balance, you need to perform regular maintenance on it, usually at least once a year. Maintenance consists of reviewing the performance of the financial securities and making changes where necessary. Over time, if you have shares that outperform the others, then their value will become too dominant in your account, upsetting the original balance that you decided upon. The usual method to rectify this or balance your portfolio is to sell some of the higher value securities and use the money to buy the under-performers, which are now less well represented in your holding. An alternative approach that avoids capital gains taxes if the portfolio is not in a tax-advantaged account is to keep hold of the good performers but direct new earnings and investments into the necessary securities. This works well if you are regularly growing the account with more savings. Once again, you can find more details on this process, including practical recommendations on how far to let the imbalance go before taking action, by studying general investment reference books.

Another item sometimes overlooked is that needs change over time, and sometimes your portfolio may need a larger overhaul. This might happen if your plans change to embrace earlier or later retirement, if you are made redundant in a poor economy, if you change your plans about having a family or become a grandparent, or marry/divorce/remarry. Many life events can be a reason to review your holdings distribution and consider rebalancing for a different emphasis.

Green Investing

You are probably familiar with general investing guidelines, and if you are not, you can refer to many sources of information to find out about them. When considering green or cleantech investment, you need to be aware of some particular issues. First, because cleantech is in many respects an emerging market, many of the companies you will consider investing in do not have a long track record. Although this is part

of the excitement of being involved in green stocks, it means you may be unable to assess the value of the company using conventional methods. Excitement can equate to risk, and you understandably might want to control risk in your portfolio. Many of these small companies will still be at a stage where they are not generating any income, as happened with the dot-com companies ten years ago, and if you were involved in investing at that time, you will recognize the dangers. Thus, you may be unable to apply ratios such as the P/E.

Other companies may not even be at this stage and simply may have "good ideas," a.k.a. untested technologies, or are still researching the technologies. Typically, this can result in high and sometimes almost uncontrolled expenditures, and if the company is not careful, it can use up its seed capital before it has a workable prototype and easily go bankrupt. The other danger if you are involved at this early stage of development is that the company will need to raise additional money, and this would have the effect of diluting any investment you have made.

Many clean-tech developments are, by their nature, at a stage when it is impossible to say whether they will be the prevailing technology in 20 or 30 years time; this is why the basic principles are outlined, and you should keep a passing familiarity, at least, with the technical aspects. If nothing else, you know that cleantech, though it may become the way of the future, must compete with conventional and often cheaper technologies in the meantime. Conventional industries have significant inertia from their long experience and will put up a fight against new ideas in which they are not involved. This means competition will come not only from other green developments, but also from the establishment.

That said, there are competing technologies within the clean sphere that will be outlined generally in this book, for example, the competition between corn-based ethanol and cellulosic ethanol, competing methods of producing ethanol. Even in the realm of biofuels, there is no certainty that ethanol will prevail against, for instance, biodiesel. All these factors add to the level of competition and consequently, the risks of green investing, even without considering the efficiencies and business acumen of individual companies that manufacture ethanol from the same process. This means the green investor must exercise particular care in making decisions.

Sometimes it is easy to see that an alternative technology is technically superior, but again, this does not mean it is a better investment. History is littered with examples of better-performing products that fell to better marketing or other commercial factors. You have only to reflect on the VHS v. Betamax or the Microsoft° v. Apple° battles to see that (at least purportedly) better products do not always capture the larger market. There are many other factors, known and unknown to the investor, that will decide the future path of greentech.

When you are reviewing clean-tech companies for their worthiness in your portfolio, it is important not to become blindsided by the idea of green investing. These companies still have to function in a commercial world, and that requires an experienced and reputable management team rather than research scientists in charge. Often, the worst person to be running a company will be the inventor of a process because he or she will be far too closely linked emotionally to the invention to necessarily make good decisions.

Depending on the stage of development, the company should have a clear idea of its marketing plan and how the product will be positioned in the industry. In most cases, it is unrealistic to think the product is so good that it will capture the market straightaway, and any claims to this effect should be viewed with suspicion. With such a fast-moving marketplace, you normally should expect that a company would have a heavier commitment to continual product development than a conventional producer, so higher than normal R&D allocations should be expected. The research should include not just the current type of product but also reviewing the up-and-coming alternatives in order to be prepared should the market shift. For example, companies that are producing conventional solar panels should spend some of their time and money keeping up with thin-film technologies.

While on this topic, if any exotic materials are required for the mass production, you need to review the security of the supply. A solar panel manufacturer using silicon technology should have good lines of supply and preferably long-term contracts with silicon producers. Particularly in an expanding industry, prices of these basic materials can fluctuate wildly with the increasing demand, and this can affect profitability dramatically.

If relevant to the product being manufactured, for example, because of a unique or novel application, it is important to know what holds the company may have over its processes. It is possible that the company can be a leader in its technical field and maintain that lead, but it is a more comfortable situation if there is a patentable process that is key to the product, and the company holds the intellectual rights. In fact, this often can make a small company a target for a takeover by a giant just to get the rights to the technology, and this can give the investor a welcome bonus as the company taking over will usually have to pay a higher than market price for the shares.

Sometimes you can see from the interest of larger companies or even venture capitalists that a small company has a potentially worthwhile product. Small companies can partner with larger corporations in order to ramp up their resources for further research and expertise, and if you find a company in this position, it is a reasonable assumption that the corporation has assessed the technology before agreeing to team up. Venture capitalists may, by their nature, be more inclined to take bigger risks than you would with your personal portfolio, but it is their business to assess worthwhile investments, and they spend a lot of time and money researching before they invest. Although this is to some extent allowing others to do the due diligence you should be doing for yourself, they have the technical expertise and funding to assess new developments in much more detail than you are probably capable of, so it can point you in the right direction.

The aspect of venture capital is one you need to study carefully. Venture capitalists often are useful to a developing company, as they have contacts throughout the industry and can arrange joint ventures and other collaborations. However, it should not be assumed that the technologies venture capitalists support are automatically going to be successes just because they have done their research. There are many different venture capitalists with their individual abilities, strengths, and weaknesses, and it would be worth reviewing how many successful clean-tech companies have been supported by the venture capitalists in question.

Another way you could look at the emerging companies in which you are considering investing is by tracking the money flow from several aspects. The actual amount of money a startup company raises is not as important as the types of money. In fact, if a startup raises too much money, it can help cover any fundamental problems and create an atmosphere that does not nurture efficiency in operation. Of far more interest is how much money the founders of the company have seen fit to put into it and whether they have convinced friends and family to contribute. Although the founders may be acting in a misguided manner from their enthusiasm for the technology, the fact that they have their own money invested will make them try harder to make a success.

A further measure of the technology is whether the company has received government grants. This is no guarantee of success, as the government can fund the technologies that do not work out in the end, though the existence of a grant implies there is some validity to the idea. Grants tend to be given more at the research stage, which is a little early for most individual investors, so it is acceptable to search for a seasoned grant when you are looking at putting money into the company. The great thing about government grants is that they do not dilute private investment and venture capital, as the government will not ask for a stake in the company, just the possibility of using the technology being developed.

Foreign investing

As you will find when you research the possibilities, with green and clean-tech investing, you are more likely to be looking internationally than you may otherwise for traditional investing. This can be an area where the typical American investor has little experience, but it need not prove a problem if you know what to do when a company is not even listed on the U.S. exchanges.

The first approach is to find a broker who has expanded the markets that they deal in outside the continental U.S. This is happening increasingly nowadays as the market for international transactions is growing. One example of such a dealer is Interactive Brokers (**www.interactivebrokers. com**), which is used by many professional traders and investment companies but is open to the individual. They boast electronic access to ninety market centers in nineteen countries, and have been around under various names since 1977.

Other brokers can offer a more bespoke service. For instance, Charles Schwab (**www.schwab.com**) supports global investing, but suggests you talk with their global investing specialist if you want to place a transaction. These deals are typically done over the phone, and Schwab takes care of the foreign exchange conversions, even offering limit orders calculated to U.S. dollar prices.

These are the ways to enter the international markets directly, but you also can find a limited number of firms who "come to you," rather than you having to seek them out. Major foreign companies sometimes are listed on the U.S. exchanges by a process called American Depository Receipt (ADR), and these have ADR appended to the stock ticker symbol. For example, international resource company BHP Billiton (**www.bhpbilliton. com**), based out of Australia and England, is quoted on the U.S. market as an ADR. The term means that a U.S. interest, probably a bank, has purchased a block of the international shares and reissued them on the U.S. markets where they can be more accessible to American investors and traders. To be able to list in this way, the company has to conform to the Securities and Exchange Commission's rules for accounting and reporting, so only the major players will take the time to comply.

Even if the company does not have an ADR listing, it may still be tradable in the U.S. by being listed on the "pink sheets." Called this because they originally were printed on pink paper (now they are mainly electronic) the pink sheets stocks are traded "over-the-counter" and not on the exchanges. These stocks, if based on U.S. companies, are typically more thinly traded and perhaps do not meet the requirements of the SEC to be listed on an exchange. When foreign companies are listed on the pink sheets, these limitations do not necessarily apply. An example of a pink sheet listing of a foreign company would be Lynas Corporation Ltd., which deals in rare earth metals and is headquartered in Sydney, Australia. It trades under the ticker LYSCF.PK. Foreign stocks usually are five letters long, finishing in "F," and the suffix PK refers to the pink sheet listing.

Depending on how you choose or are able to trade the foreign stocks, you should watch out for fees. First, if the stock is not directly accessible, there may be intermediary dealers, each of whom will rack up a commission for their involvement, making the fees higher and requiring a greater profit on the shares just to break even. The good news is that an increasing number of U.S. brokers are adding foreign trading capabilities to their services. The Securities and Exchange Commission also is looking at easing the restrictions on foreign-based brokers offering accounts in the U.S., which may lead to cost saving competition.

Investing in Green Funds

Instead of directing your investments into individual stocks and shares, you may want to consider buying into some "green funds." This is a popular and expanding market, but just because a fund is labeled "green" does not make it worthy of investment or indeed necessarily green in the terms that are expressed in this book. You still need to perform your own assessment or trust someone else to have your best interests at heart and look after your money as well as you would.

The advantage of investing via a fund is that you have a professional fund manager whose job it is to keep track of how the investments are performing and with the expertise to select what should be the best assets for your portfolio. Because a fund has more money than an individual, it also may have access to financial instruments that a single investor could not use. However, just because the fund has a professional steering the funds does not guarantee that your money will be put to the "best" use, as it will come down to the expertise and foresight of the manager.

Although many people think of mutual funds, as they have been around the longest, several different types of funds are available nowadays, each with slight differences. The mutual fund started nearly a century ago in the U.S., just in time for the stock market crash, which was not good timing. In the next couple of decades, various laws passed, mainly because of the crash, which imposed more regulations. This was a good thing, as it gives investors more protections.

Mutual funds can be either open-end or closed-end. Closed-end funds have a set amount of shares in the fund, and the price can vary away from the value of the holdings. Open-end funds are more usual, and the price (net asset value or NAV) is calculated after the markets close to exactly match to the value of the company shares that the fund holds. If more investors come in to the fund, then the fund manager buys more company shares. It is a collective holding of many different companies' shares, and you can check the prospectus to see what the fund invests in.

If you are interested in looking at mutual funds for some of your portfolio, then there are a number of points you have to check. The funds have to pay their staff, the fund manager, and office expenses, so while you can calculate the value directly from the holdings or look at the NAV each day and know exactly what your investment is worth, you will be charged a percentage each year to cover their costs. This can be anything from a fraction of a percent up to several percent, and as it is charged each year, it is worth finding a fund with a lower fee.

Funds also can make money by charging when you invest in them; this is called a "load." With competition, it is possible to find funds that do not charge a load, and they are called "no-load" funds. Most studies show that funds with loads do not perform noticeably better than no-load funds, and it comes down to individual fund selection. Be aware that some funds impose a "back-end" load, that is, a fee when you sell your position. Again, you can select funds that do not have this penalty.

Several types of funds are available, even beyond selecting a market sector or the size of the company. You can find funds that target foreign or local companies, which try to emulate the performance of an index, such as the Dow Jones Industrial Average (DJIA), and many other variables. There is much more information available in reference books and online, both free and paid services such as the much-respected Morningstar (**www.morningstar.com**).

The other generally used fund is the exchange-traded fund (ETF), a relatively modern fund only introduced in the past twenty years. The underlying idea is to group many investors together, as with a mutual fund, but the difference is, as the name suggests, ETFs are traded on an exchange while the market is open and can be bought and sold just like shares. They started out as index funds but are available in other forms, which multiply or invert the performance of an index, for example. They rapidly have become a popular alternative to the mutual fund.

List of popular funds

For your convenience, if you decide not to invest in individual companies, here is a list of popular "green" funds. As always, you must do your own research into whether you want to put your money into any of them, and this list gives you a starting point. It cannot be exhaustive, as the green fund field is growing, but it will give you plenty of scope to start with. *This list is also available for reference in Appendix A.*

All these funds concentrate on the environmental side when choosing their investments. There are many other "socially responsible" funds, which include other aspects such as animal testing, weapons, tobacco, etc., in their selection, as well as the clean-tech industries, so there are fewer "pure play" funds than you might think — although if you feel strongly about those other aspects, too, you might want to research that side of the funds further at **www.morningstar.com** or another financial site.

There are many aspects when choosing a fund to invest in, and you can find more details in *The Mutual FundsBook — How to Invest in Mutual Funds & Earn High Rates of Return Safely*, also published by Atlantic Publishing.

HERE IS A LIST OF GREEN MUTUAL FUNDS:

Acuity Clean Environment Equity (ACUITYCLEANE.TO)

Alger Green Fund (SPEGX)

Appleseed Fund (APPLX)

Calvert Global Alternative Energy (CGAEX)

Calvert Global Water Fund (CFWAX)

Calvert International Equity (CWGVX)

Calvert International Opportunities (CWVYX)

Calvert Large Cap Growth (CLGAX)

Calvert Moderate Allocation (CMAAX)

Calvert Small Cap Fund (CCVAX)

Calvert Social Index (CSXAX)

Claymore S&P Global Water Index (ETF:CWWA:TO)

CRA Qualified Investment (CRATX)

Domini International Social Equity (DOMAX)

Domini Social Equity (DSEPX)

ESG Managers Aggressive Growth Portfolio (PAGAX)

First Trust NASDAQ Clean Edge US (ETF: QCLN)

First Trust ISE Water Index Fund (ETF: FIW)

Gabelli SRI Green mutual fund (SRIAX)

Green Century Balanced (GCBLX)

Green Century Equity (GCEQX)

Guinness Atkinson Alternative Energy (GAAEX)

Legg Mason Investment Counsel Social Awareness (SSIAX)

Market Vectors Environmental Services ETF (EVX)

Market Vectors Global Alternative Energy ETF (GEX)

Market Vectors Solar Energy ETF (KWT)

New Alternatives Fund (NALFX)

PFW Water ETF (PFWAX)

Parnassus Equity Income (PRBLX)

Parnassus Fixed Income (PRFIX)

Parnassus Fund (PARNX)

Parnassus Mid-Cap Fund (PARMX)

Parnassus Small-Cap Fund (PARSX)

Parnassus Workplace Fund (PARWX)

Pax World Balanced Fund (PAXWX)

Pax World Global Green Fund (PGRNX)

Pax World Growth Fund (PXWGX)

Pax World High Yield Bond Fund (PAXHX)

Pax World International Fund (PXINX)

Pax World Small Cap Fund (PXSCX)

Pax World Womens Equity Fund (PXWEX)

Portfolio 21 (PORTX)

PowerShares Cleantech Portfolio (ETF:PZD)

PowerShares Global Water Portfolio (ETF: PIO)

PowerShares Water Resource (ETF: PHO)

PowerShares WilderHill Clean Energy (ETF: PBW)

PowerShares WilderHill Progressive Energy (ETF: PUW)

Sentinel Sustainable Core Opportunities (MYPVX)

Sentinel Sustainable Growth Opportunities (WAEGX)

Wells Fargo Advantage Social Sustainability Fund (WSSAX)

Winslow Green Growth (WGGFX)

Chapter 3

What Does
Green Mean?

efore considering the different types of green and clean technology worthy of investment, it is a good idea to define what "green" means, particularly as it seems to be one of those catchwords many companies throw around in an attempt to look modern and investable. Companies can make money by appearing to be environmentally responsible, and in some cases, they might do so by the simple process of an attention-getting advertising campaign. After all, it is possible to claim a carbon-neutral business either by cleaning up the operation or by obtaining credit for tree planting in another part of the world to offset existing carbon dioxide emissions that have not been reduced.

The generally accepted meaning of green technology is that it embraces processes that are environmentally responsible and do not degrade our world in the same way as traditional processes. The sometimes-contested area is that when any action is performed, there is a change in the surroundings so nothing is totally neutral to the environment. To be environmentally responsible, it is necessary to cut or eliminate harmful waste and pollutants and use renewable energy and materials. At the very least, companies must cut down on how many natural resources they consume.

Included in this brief are all types of energy, transportation of people and goods, clean water, and alternative or green materials, all of which are discussed in turn in the following chapters. For several decades, green has been considered an expensive alternative to the conventional way of doing things, and for good reason. It is only recently that developments have allowed green technology to become competitive in the marketplace and to become so accepted that it has the support and subsidies from big government. Although many people would like businesses and corporations to act in what they regard as a moral manner, what often is forgotten is that businesses exist to earn and maximize their profits. There is little room for a social conscience in business, as the competitor who does not exhibit this has been able to drive the ecologically aware corporation out of business. The primary duty of a board of directors is to make sure that profits and dividends are maintained or increased so the price of the stocks will not fall and shareholders will not move their money elsewhere.

Most recently, the necessity of environmentally aware decision making has become evident and has combined with the technological ability to make green investment worthwhile. In many cases, cleantech is being developed to the point of providing solutions as cheaply as traditional methods. In some senses, this is a revolution that will impact where and how we live, as well as the products we create, buy, and use. The revolution is real as states impose their own mandates on pollution and using clean technology. This encompasses such matters as the amount of electricity derived from renewable sources by a specific target year. California is typically a leader among states in pushing an environmental agenda. Electricity consumers often are given the choice of electing to use green power, even if it is slightly more expensive, and this helps subsidize what has been a heavier price for the supply company.

As this is written, there is the dawn of realistic hybrid and electric energy motor vehicles. It started on a small scale and was priced at a premium in 2003, but over the years and with government tax incentives, the energy-efficient car has become a genuine option for those seeking to replace their conventional vehicles. As hybrid production increases and prices fall, the future of oil and gasoline is looking increasingly expensive, and many of the mainstream public will make a conscious decision to support green technology.

USCAP

Inevitably, there have been obstacles as companies adopt green processes. The United States Climate Action Partnership (USCAP) was formed in 2007, with many large companies deciding to cooperate and lobby government for regulations that require significant reductions in greenhouse gas emissions. By encouraging legislation, these large companies were ensuring they were not disadvantaged compared with their competitors by taking steps toward cleaner processes, and the USCAP actions would result in all companies needing to take on the costs of reducing emissions. This act of voluntarily encouraging regulations affecting how companies operate shows the extent to which green has entered the corporate world.

Unfortunately, all did not go smoothly, and in February 2010, three companies, BP, Conoco Phillips, and Caterpillar announced they would not renew their membership.

To some extent, this was a reaction to the political climate, which made it seem unlikely that the government would enact the legislation in the near future. More than 20 other large companies, including Royal Dutch Shell, GE, and Honeywell, continued the coalition's efforts. For its part, BP had made a conscious decision in 2000 to show it was committed to alternative energy when it starting changing its image by adopting the name BP rather than British Petroleum and claiming that "BP" stood for "Beyond Petroleum." Despite this, most of its money still comes from the oil business.

It would be idealistic to suggest that companies are prepared to go away from the idea of maximizing their profits in order to make their businesses greener. As previously mentioned, companies are established to obtain the maximum profit and might not last in the commercial marketplace if they concentrate too much on environmental issues. It is rumored that BP found it could save more than $650 million by reducing its carbon dioxide emissions in conjunction with changing its image to the environmentally friendlier "Beyond Petroleum." This change serves to demonstrate how green issues are now not only environmentally desirable but also can be profitable.

It also highlights the changes from what may have applied in the past about green technology. In the early days of environmentally friendly technology, not only was it more expensive than conventional technology, but also small startup companies spearheaded the environmentally friendly movement, typically with entrepreneur inventors at their heads. These people saw that alternatives could be found, and that in the future they would need to be found. Nowadays, large corporations with deep pockets also are finding that green technology is a worthwhile investment, and this means there are mainstream profits to be made.

Non-Green Power Sources

To further elucidate what green means, it is necessary to define what it does not mean. The following represent some conventional sources of energy that are not considered green.

Nuclear power

The Sequoyah nuclear power plant in Tennessee

Nuclear power is not green. Although it can enjoy a brief revival while the emphasis is on reducing carbon dioxide emissions, the suggestion to use radioactive materials, which currently have no environmentally friendly disposal method, is absurd. Not only are the radioactive materials dangerous in and of themselves, but also the nuclear material can be refined and used to create weapons that are appalling in their outcome. Every nuclear power plant, as part of its normal operation, produces plutonium by a fission process, and plutonium and/or highly enriched uranium, the original fuel for a reactor, is an essential ingredient for a nuclear bomb. Periodically, "spent" fuel rods containing plutonium must be removed and replaced.

Putting aside the issue of radioactivity, nuclear power plants require large amounts of materials, particularly concrete, to construct and large amounts of water to cool their reactors while they are operating. This became evident in 2005 when France, long considered a model for nuclear power, was unable to maintain capacity from its generating plants safely because of drought conditions. Without an adequate water supply, nuclear power plants can overheat and melt down. As France depends heavily on nuclear power for its electricity, in order to overcome the problem there are plans to build underwater nuclear reactors that would be moored offshore. No doubt this, will present many new environmental issues the engineers will have to address, but the matter of safety for such a novel application must be a concern. Recent events in Japan have shown that the Earth has little regard for what man declares to be the worst-case design criteria, so even the soundest of designs may fail, even assuming no human errors are made. The prototype is due to be completed by 2016. Despite this being a possible solution to reactor cooling for countries with coastal regions, it does not present any resolution to the other issues with using nuclear power.

On March 11, 2011, Japan suffered a massive earthquake, which was beyond the structural limitations of the design of its nuclear plant at Fukushima. From this and the ensuing tsunami, there have been significant radiation leaks. In April, the operator of the power plant stated it would take six to nine months to achieve "cold shutdown" of the plant, and at the end of July, they were still transferring radioactive water to a containment facility. On May 30, 2011, the German government announced its decision to shut down all nuclear power plants by 2022. It immediately closed eight of its seventeen facilities, those that were not operational for various reasons, including shutdown for testing following the Japanese disaster as well as for maintenance. With a quarter of its electricity dependent on nuclear power, this well-intentioned gut reaction will cause significant problems for the world's fourth largest economy. However, Chancellor Angela Merkel was adamant that the decision would be irrevocable and that it provided an excellent opportunity for Germany. By 2025, Germany hopes to double its clean-technology percentage, creating jobs and helping the environment. Germany is still somewhat dependent on coal-fired plants; so, ironically, the action will cause a spike in emissions as they are used to satisfy the needs.

Unfortunately, a report from the Economist Intelligence Unit suggests that not all countries have taken the lesson so seriously. The report, entitled *The Future of Nuclear Energy*, suggests there will be a 27-percent growth in output from nuclear plants by 2020. The reactors already planned for China, India, and Russia alone will more than make up for the German decision, adding five times as much nuclear capacity as Germany has eliminated. Of course, because of the time it takes to build a nuclear facility, much of this was already underway when disaster struck Fukushima.

The United States had a long period where no new nuclear power plants were envisaged. In fact, the last two construction starts were in 1973 and 1974, and the only one from that era still continuing undergoing construction is in Tennessee, which was completed in 2012. However, during the 21st century, there has been a renaissance in the industry, and various projects with subsidies and other government assistance have been started. Although nuclear power claims a lower operating cost than some conventional generating plants, the cost of construction is prohibitive and only can be justified by government assistance with loan guarantees and insurance help. The nuclear industry proudly boasts an impressive safety record, but considering the deleterious consequences if safety failed, this is perhaps the least we should expect.

Coal

Another industry that makes claim to being green is "clean coal." At the present time, this is a misnomer. Clean coal, which describes the process of burning coal so it does not pollute, does not exist; methods to burn coal that eliminate carbon dioxide emissions, and other pollutants that make "acid rain" are expensive, experimental, and, in many cases, provide only a limited answer, as, for example, storing the pollutants underground. Coal is a

cheap way to generate much of the electricity used in the United States, so it has many advocates. There is no commercial method that would eliminate the carbon dioxide emissions produced when it burns, and it will be some years at least before the burning of coal in a non-polluting manner is commercially viable and capable of general implementation.

There are several problems with burning coal. The most prominent might be the carbon dioxide emissions, but other pollutants such as sulfur dioxide can cause acid rain when released into the atmosphere. Various techniques have been proposed to deal with the totality of these issues, none of which has reached a commercially viable development stage. Some of these techniques involve chemical washing of the gaseous combustion products, treating them with steam, or capturing the pollutants and storing them underground.

There is one "clean coal" power plant in the world, in Germany, and this is state-owned because of the high cost of construction. The solution it uses to clean up pollutants is to capture them and compress the carbon dioxide to form a liquid. The carbon dioxide is injected into depleted gas fields for storage. Inevitably, this does not present a long-term sustainable solution.

One process that seems to offer hope in the future is the gasification of coal, which would break down coal into various components such as natural gas and a cleaner burning fuel. However, this still would produce carbon dioxide, which is more easily captured but would have to be stored underground or underwater. It is obvious that there is a long way to go before coal is either clean or an environmentally friendly investment option.

Oil

It is plainly obvious to most observers that oil is an unsustainable and ecologically unsound method of generating energy. The fact that significant industries, such as motoring, have been built around and depend on it for basic operation merely means it will take some time before it can be eliminated or morphed into a better alternative.

As we will look at later, renewable substitutes have a place, even though continuing with the basic scheme of burning fuels produces, at least, carbon dioxide emissions that must be offset for a sustainable future.

CASE STUDY: COMMITTED TO ETHICAL INVESTING

Ron Robins, MBA
Founder
Investing for the Soul
7625 Ronnie Crescent
Niagara Falls, ON Canada L2G 7M1
289-271-0873
www.investingforthesoul.com
ronr@investingforthesoul.com

Mr. Robins is founder of the globally popular and respected ethical investing site, Investing for the Soul; writes the Enlightened Economics blog about a new economics integrating consciousness, natural law, and free-market theory; and is a financial and economics columnist for alrroya.com, a leading Middle Eastern business publication and portal (http://alrroya.com).

Beginning in 1969, Mr. Robins held investment industry positions in securities analysis, OTC trading, and global private equity sales. During the 1990s, he was regarded as North America's most successful marketer and instructor of the Transcendental Meditation (TM) technique to financial executives. His education includes business and spiritual studies at institutions of higher learning in the United Kingdom, Switzerland, Canada, and the United States. Among his many qualifications are an MBA degree and Honours standing in the Canadian Securities Course.

I am involved in green investing in a number of ways. I first began engaging in this topic in the mid-1970s when a colleague and I tried to create a Canadian ethical fund. I am also founder of, and analyst, at Investing for the Soul (**www.investingforthesoul.com**), which according to Google rankings is one of the world's premier green-ethical investing sites. I have been writing and commenting on green-ethical investing for more than a decade and frequently write about it in a finance and economics column for a leading Middle Eastern business publication and portal, **alrroya.com**. I also have had various green investments from as early as 1969.

My background in green investing goes back to 1969 when I entered the investment industry, beginning a career that ranged from investment analyst, over-the-counter trader, to global private equity sales. From about 1970, I became passionately committed to personal development, beginning first to practice and then by teaching the Transcendental Meditation technique to business and financial executives. Many of my associates and students were interested in aligning their personal values and ethics with their investments, which led me to ethical-green investing.

What I find most interesting about my environmentally responsible work is that it is in harmony with my values and that simultaneously, it promises outsized returns. I perceived back in the 1970s that this is where most investors eventually will wind up. It was clear to me then that the world was going headlong into an ecological disaster, and therefore, many investment opportunities would open up in the green-ethical investing space as humanity awoke to dealing with this extraordinary issue.

The biggest problem I see in my work is still the intransigence of most investment advisers. It is their lack of understanding of green-ethical investing and their frequent unwillingness to bring up the subject with their clients. Their clients on the other hand are usually interested in the subject but, for fear of looking foolish, fail to bring it up to their adviser.

My work and outlook has not changed because of the global recession, as I had prepared for it and for what I believe is coming in the next decade. I had been expecting the global recession for many years. It has been obvious to me that overall debt levels in most developed world economies had been growing annually 50 percent to 150 percent faster than GDP or income growth since the early 1980s. It was just a matter of time before investors observed the unsustainable onerous debt levels and took action. Thus, the global recession hit, and I am still expecting much worse yet as our addiction to excessive debt to finance growth and consumption has not changed. Primarily, I am an ethical investor, and the ethics behind central banks and governments pushing — like drug dealers — ever more amounts of debt I deem unethical and deceitful. In this context, I have been a believer that governments and central banks will attempt to inflate away their debt. As this occurs, huge funds will flow into commodities that will lift all energy prices. As energy prices rise and the need to cope with climate change becomes ever more apparent, green stocks could do well in the years ahead. Also, I believe rising trade frictions will create trade and tariff barriers, reinforcing the development of local green renewable energy and technological systems.

The qualities I believe that led me to green-ethical investing include a strong sense of ethics and spirituality, plus a deep conviction that through our investing activities we can create a sustainable AND prosperous, happier world. It is my deep belief that we need to care for our environment and that we, humanity, and all existence are an interdependent whole organism with a transcendent, omnipotent consciousness that links everything in our world, both manifest and non-manifest.

The biggest challenge I have to overcome in my work is how to get people to think more deeply about their own situation, their values, the environment around them, and the world. Most people are so wrapped up in their relatively small affairs that they miss the big picture. It has been clear for decades that we have been disturbing and destroying the world's ecosystems and environment. Also, it was evident to anyone who cared to look at U.S., U.K., and European private and public debt levels leading up to 2007, that an economic catastrophe would occur. Even now, government and central bank deceit is rampant about the extent of the problem. Few bother to understand the big pictures until it impacts them directly. Deceit and denial that these problems even exist are widespread. Thus, few will act until the midnight hour of disaster occurs.

The advice I would give to someone interested in following a similar path to mine would be, above all, know what your values are and build your life and work around those values. It is immensely satisfying and rewarding to do that. And when doing what you love, you generally do well and excel. You might even make good money doing it and, ideally, benefit our whole world in the process.

Green Investment Options

Several technologies are clean and are presently developing strongly. Below is an overview of a few options available for those who are interested in making green investments. *These are discussed in detail in later chapters.*

Solar

Photovoltaic panels on the roof of a house

One of the strongest forms of developing green technology is solar energy. The most well-known application of solar energy is the photovoltaic (PV) array, typically mounted on roofs in residential applications and sometimes pictured en masse in the desert in a "solar farm." Significant progress is being made in this field. Traditional photovoltaic devices are silicon-based, heavy, and expensive, and although these are being refined, other technologies, such as thin-film and even paintable solutions, are being researched.

But mentioning only photovoltaic uses for solar energy would be missing half the benefit. From positioning buildings to admit more light and heat to the more sophisticated heat-capturing devices, such as roof-mounted collectors or Trombe walls, solar power embraces direct and indirect heating and cooling applications. *These building factors are covered in Chapter 9.* They are a different concept and technology from the photovoltaic devices.

Wind

Wind turbines

In contrast to PV devices, wind energy operates with different and more readily understood science. After all, conventional windmills have been used for centuries with the mechanical power typically used to grind cereal. Another frequent use of wind power is to drive water pumps. Even the Greeks used wind power for machines. Compared to solar energy, there are fewer areas of the country where wind power can achieve its maximum benefit, and this tends to lead to specific areas where many huge wind turbines are installed. Recent years have seen more development of smaller-scale wind projects.

Technology developing for wind power is in the design of the turbines themselves — sometimes using high-tech materials — and the control systems that ensure maximum benefit is derived from whatever the prevailing wind can provide. Generating electricity from wind power is a viable and improving technology, and countries such as Germany and Denmark have wind provide 8 and 21 percent, respectively, of their national electric power. The noted disadvantages of wind power compared with solar energy are its obtrusiveness, noise, and unpredictable intermittency.

Wave power

Wave power is power generated by the oceans, specifically by wave movements from wind, though for simplicity, tidal power is included in this category. The earth's rotation, gravity, and the moon causes tides. In either case, the actual water movement is a good source of energy, or "energy dense" as it is called; the issue is how to harness what looks like a random movement to make mechanical work, and thus generate power.

Some of the installations are out at sea, where the waves are generally stronger and more consistent; this means that the electricity has farther to travel back to shore and to its point of use. Because of this, wave power generators have to be rugged and built to withstand the harshest natural conditions. It is not likely that there ever will be a universal wind power generator design, as each installation is custom designed for the location.

Electricity

On a residential level, both solar PV power and wind power benefit from government regulations that permit the sale of excess electricity back onto the grid. By selling electricity back, the costs of installation are mitigated. This sometimes is described as the meter running backward, but it depends on how the power supplier chooses to meter the amount of surplus electricity and whether they install a sec-

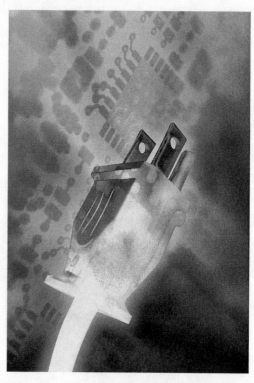

ond meter to measure it. Unlike the commercial power generator, when you are a residential customer selling back excess power generated, you are credited for power you return to the grid, and it is sold to the utility at the full consumer rate. This process is called "net metering." Although you cannot become a commercial power generator this way, it is a useful income addition to help with the cost of installation. The electricity grid provides you with a virtual "battery" you can use to store your power, and this is yet another way governmental action has made it more favorable to adopt alternative energy.

Apart from meters that run backward, the electrical grid is being revised into a smart grid the utility providers can use to optimize their power supplies. This extends far beyond being able to access power consumptions remotely, which is called remote meter reading and has been talked about for some time. Simple meter reading is a tried technology available to any utility company that considers it a worthwhile investment. In contrast, a smart grid includes controlling electricity use to avoid excess demand in peak periods; for example, controlling the time of water heating to limit the strain on the system. As you may imagine, this involves integrating vast amounts of data, which is an ideal task for computers and will evolve as regulations are developed for interconnecting the grid to the consumer.

Geothermal

Although solar and wind applications generally are well accepted by the public, a more contentious issue is geothermal energy. This again has great potential, with heat from the Earth's core accessed via wells and brought to the surface, typically to drive electric generating equipment. Sometimes geothermal energy also is accessed for direct heating purposes. In either case, there has been discussion about possible contamination of any water brought to the surface and then recirculated and of the possible seismic effects of localized underground cooling. Most recently, buried heat transmission pipes that do not involve water transfer have been developed, and these take care of some of the concerns.

Water

An estimated 1 billion people on this planet do not have reliable access to clean water. Apart from any concerns about an impending shortage of water in the Western world, this is also a matter of social and humanitarian importance, and more methods are being developed to deploy clean technologies for water purification and filtration. There are two different problems here — in some cases there is a physical shortage of water, and in others it is a matter of a lack of technology to make water safe and drinkable, such as by using desalination plants to purify seawater.

Technology has once again improved the situation. In contrast to traditional methods, nanotechnology has been developed to enable water that was once considered unusable to be filtered and purified. Although water filtration is not necessarily the answer to the shortage of drinking water in the deserts of the southwestern states, it certainly can be used in developing countries, not only for seawater desalination but also for making otherwise undrinkable supplies into usable water for drinking and agricultural purposes.

Building

Turning now to buildings, there has been rapid progress in recent years to make new buildings green as typified in the LEED program, which set certain standards for all building elements. Savings of at least 30 percent have been realized in the energy consumption, and when green is planned from the inception of the building construction, it often costs little more than conventional buildings. One side benefit of building green is that it often results in a more beneficial internal environment, for instance by monitoring controlled parameters more closely and introducing more outside air, which in offices will result in greater productivity and better staff retention. The elements of green building have been available for some time, with increasingly sophisticated building management systems to control the building engineering for example, but the LEED program forces building professionals to consider the building holistically and ensure all adopted measures are integrated to work in concert with each other.

Transportation

In the field of transportation, and, in particular, personal transportation, great strides have been made since the original Toyota˚ Prius was introduced several years ago. The Prius was the first mass-produced hybrid electric car, introduced in 1997 into its home market of Japan. The Honda Insight was the first on the U.S. market, but, arguably, the Prius has been much more successful. In addition to hybrid vehicles, which combine electric drive and gasoline motors, the all-electric vehicle is becoming a practical possibility. Their range has been improving with advanced battery technology, although there is still the question of how to make long trips in such a vehicle. Some plan that charged batteries will be available to swap out at refueling stations, while others are trying to solve the problem using quick-charging techniques. It is not clear what technology may be triumphant, but it is certain that whatever option wins will have a huge market in a few years.

Unlike Europe, where gasoline has been prohibitively expensive for many years, the U.S. has not faced up to the need to drive smaller personal vehicles, and the prevailing trend until recently has been for larger and heavier transportation, as typified in the SUV truck. Part of the prevailing wisdom has been that, if involved in an accident, the driver would prefer to be protected by a big and weighty structure rather than driving a lightweight, small, economical vehicle. However, the current world conditions mandate that even in the U.S., steps should be taken to reduce or eliminate oil dependency.

The particular challenge the U.S. faces is that, unlike many other countries, it has little viable public transportation in all but some of the most concentrated metro areas. The predominant dependency on personal vehicles makes it more difficult to come up with uniform and collective answers to environmentally friendly ways of getting around. One area of expansion may be biofuels. In Brazil, for example, more than 80 percent of automobile fuels are manufactured from plants, with ethanol made from sugar cane. The ethanol from corn debacle already has been mentioned, with fuel needs competing with the need for food, but several other crops, which are discussed later, may be easier to grow and do not take away from food production.

Doing your own research

Investing in green technology can mean many things. It is possible to find investments at many different stages of development, and this book does not seek to recommend specific companies or endorse investing in them. Companies will be named as examples, but it is a fast-moving topic, and by the time you read about them they already may have peaked or even lost their momentum. None of the companies should be regarded as investable without you doing your own independent investigation and assuring yourself that they will meet your goals, objectives, and propensity for risk.

In addition to mentioning companies and the factors to consider when selecting your environmentally friendly investments, the following chapters elaborate on the engineering and technology involved in realizing the future in each class of green knowledge. In this way, you will be best prepared to understand the importance of any discoveries you may find reported and have a better sense of how advanced the business is so you can assess the investment risks.

Chapter 4

Solar Power

olar energy is an exciting prospect that the present government intends to expand greatly. In fact, President Obama announced on May 2014 that solar panels and solar heating were now operational in the White House. The White House previously used solar panels, which were installed by the Carter administration in 1979, but then removed them in a re-roofing project under Reagan in 1986. Solar was reinstated under Bush, just to serve an outbuilding and swimming pool. In 2012, 7.6 percent of the U.S. electrical supply came from renewable resources. This seems like a bright future for solar power, and the way it has caught the public imagination, one would think that in a few years conventional power plants will be phased out in its favor.

To inject a little realism here, the government publishes figures of the national power supply and how much is derived from each source. You can find these on the website of the U.S. Energy Information Administration (**www.eia.doe.gov**). By the end of 2014, the latest figures available at the time of writing, total electrical generation for the nation, was 4,500,491 kilo watt-hrs. Of this, about 360,000 kilo watt-hrs came from renewables, including wood, municipal waste and landfill gas, geothermal, wind, biomass, and solar. If you work that out, it means just less than 8 percent of all power came from all these renewables put together.

If you delve deeper, the net generation from solar thermal and photovoltaic sources was 891,000 megawatt-hrs, which works out to a fraction of a percent of the power the U.S. uses. It is astonishing that solar power has captured the public imagination so much that it can be spoken of in election promises, and yet doubling the capacity would not provide a noticeable impact on our nation's electricity supply.

Although this may be a sad revelation for those who thought solar power was on the verge of making a breakthrough against burning fossil fuels, the other side of this truth is that the market is wide open for increasing solar power installations. Therefore, the companies that are successful in the technology will undergo great expansion and provide the associated investment opportunities, which fundamentally is what you are reading this book for. But you also need to take into account that the solar power industry in the U.S. may be somewhat lagging compared to other countries.

Factors that will ensure investors benefit from solar power sales include a 30-percent investment tax credit for solar installations, which, at time of writing, will apply at least until 2016. This federal personal tax credit applies to new residential solar-electric and solar hot water installations (except swimming pools and hot tubs) with no maximum limit. The American Economic Recovery Act also included funding that would benefit the solar industry.

Solar Power Electricity

The principal focus on adopting solar as a renewable energy resource has been on photovoltaic panels, which generate electricity when exposed to the sun. Astonishingly, the basic idea for the modern solar panel has been around since 1954 when a researcher at Bell Labs who was experimenting with semiconductors noted that silicon with some impurities was sensitive to light. Bell Labs went on to create the first practical solar cell with an efficiency of several percentage points. Efficiency is measured by the amount of energy present in the light striking the solar cell and how much is converted to electrical power.

But Bell Labs did not discover the principle of generating power from light, called the photoelectric effect. In 1839, a Frenchman named Edmond Becquerel was experimenting with an early electric battery and first noted the photoelectric effect. The next experiment was 37 years later, when William Grylls Adams discovered that the element selenium would produce electricity when exposed to light. In 1883, the American inventor Charles

Fritts produced what is thought to be the first real solar cell, even though it was less than 1 percent efficient, from wafers of selenium coated with gold.

Most solar photovoltaic panels are made using silicon, and this is an expensive component. For manufacturers of what are now considered conventional PV panels, the focus is on increasing the efficiency of the panels and in reducing the amount of silicon used for each. The current energy conversion rate is about 18 percent, so there is scope for improvement. If there is a breakthrough, it is likely that the company that makes it will gain market share.

The other way in which solar panel manufacturers can compete is by expansion, which would allow greater economies of scale and more competitive pricing. For all companies with a working production line, expansion is possible given the public attention and the subsidies available, thus capital acquisition and utilization will be an important factor.

For a few years, companies have sought an alternative to the heavy and expensive silicon-based solar photovoltaic panels. Various materials have been tried with varying degrees of success, and many of them fall under the general title of "thin-film solar cells" because they are much thinner than the conventional panels. If these ever become mainstream, it is likely that conventional panels will decline in popularity because of their weight and bulk, even though with a life of perhaps 25 years, you will be seeing silicon panels in use for many years to come.

Thin-film PV cells use layers of semiconductor materials less than 1/1000 of an inch thick that are deposited onto inexpensive materials such as glass or even flexible plastic. At present, thin films are approximately 8 percent efficient, but in many uses, the efficiency is not the only criteria, and a larger area can be tolerated. From a consumer's point of view, cost is also a large factor. The materials used for thin film vary and include cadmium telluride, copper indium gallium selenide, and other exotically named substances. However, because of the small amount of material used in the thin-film cells, they can be much cheaper than the silicon-based units. Some manufacturers of silicon-based units have tried to compete by using reflector arrays that concentrate sunlight onto small chips of silicon, but at present this seems unlikely to become a popular choice because the arrays need to be motorized and continually pointed at the sun for the system to work, adding to complication and cost. Thin film currently accounts for 25 percent of the solar energy market.

A third type of solar panel is the "building integrated photovoltaic panel." Most of these use a type of silicon called amorphous that is mounted on industrial fabric rather than using the crystalline silicon of conventional panels. A typical example of these panels is a type of roofing shingle that makes the panel effectively disappear into the construction. These models are not quite as easy to apply as roofing shingles, as they incorporate electrodes that have to be fed through holes in the roof structure, but considering that roofing shingles would need to be applied in any construction, these panels can save on labor.

The main problem with the building-integrated panels is that they tend to get hot. Because they are mounted directly on the building structure, there is no air gap for cooling circulation, and this means their efficiency of energy production is reduced compared to the other methods. It remains to be seen whether using alternate construction materials that have the benefit of producing power will prove viable.

Solar Heat

So far, we only have considered generating electricity with sun power. This is the form of solar power most commonly thought of when the topic is discussed. But for many years, the sun has been used to heat homes naturally, and various methods have been devised, depending on the prevailing climate, to capture and use the sun's heat. Just as a greenhouse can be much warmer than the outside temperature, so, too, can installing windows at the appropriate orientation help capture the sun's heat.

One of the inventions available to harvest the sun's energy is called the Trombe wall, named after a Frenchman who popularized (but did not invent) the concept. In its most fundamental form, the Trombe wall is really just heavy construction, often using concrete, and because heat goes through concrete at the rate of about 1 inch per hour, an 8-inch concrete wall will release a proportion of the heat it received (the rest being reradiated to the outside) into a room eight hours after it receives it, which would warm a room in the evening from the morning sunlight. You can get details of the Trombe wall by searching on the Internet if you are interested, but in its basic form, it uses no specialized equipment or components, so it is not a system that benefits an investor.

One alternative arrangement is to create airspace between exterior glass and a solid wall, and to allow or force air to travel through the airspace with vents at high and low levels, which can offer temperature conditioning if a series of controls is added. Again, this may be nothing particularly exceptional for investment, but it may perhaps be of personal interest. Some variations of the Trombe wall have been tried, such as the thermal storage window or Trombe window, and there may be some inventions using the idea of thermal storage in the future.

Investing in Solar

Even when considered worldwide, solar power counts for much less than 1 percent of the world's energy. This means there is great scope for expansion for the companies that make the goods people want at a reasonable price and market them effectively. However, it may be more suitable for an investor with a long-term perspective to invest in solar power, as it will take some time to gear up to effective levels. Some pundits are suggesting that solar will be a force to be reckoned with during the next ten years because it rapidly is coming to a point of parity with conventional generating sources. CNN reports the International Energy Agency (IEA) considers solar panels will compete by 2020 and provide 5 percent of world electricity supplies by 2030.

Because it is starting from such a small market share, you can expect solar to continue at a phenomenal growth rate. The other aspect in solar's favor is that many large multinational companies have been watching the industry and taking steps to become involved. Much of the American South-

A solar-powered water heater

west has conspicuous sunshine, but solar can be effective in other areas, too. The cost barrier gradually is being eroded, and in the meantime, the subsidies and tax breaks available make going solar worth calculating and possibly a breakeven proposition.

Companies such as Citizenre (**www.citizenre.com**), RentSolar (**www.rentsolar.com**), RentalSolar (**www.rentalsolar.com**), and many others have sprung up to make solar affordable. They offer to rent equipment that is installed for free to homeowners and make promises of up to 20 percent savings monthly compared to the price of buying electricity. An additional benefit is that the rate is fixed, rather than going up every year as electricity costs tend to do. Many companies are following this business plan, and some of the companies are "distributors" for the parent companies that rent the equipment — it is generally easy to become a distributor for a solar rental company and become eligible for payments for each new client. The great majority of these companies are small and privately held, are run by would-be entrepreneurs, and are not investable.

Solar's growth rate is one of the reasons there is so much interest in the industry. Large multinational companies are determined not to be left behind, which means quite a few research dollars are at work refining the technology. The disincentives to the solar industry include the momentum of the long-term fossil fuel advocates, the variety of electrical utility power districts that makes adopting a universal standard difficult, and cost factors still to be overcome. Because of the emphasis on semiconductors in photovoltaic work, the best investment options are more likely to be electronics companies, such as Sharp and Sanyo, that are experienced with semiconductors rather than the traditional energy companies, such as Shell and BP, that are taking an interest but have less electronics experience.

A measure of competitiveness

Although solar is nearly at the breakthrough level, subsidies are required to hasten its adoption. Where there is a choice of buying a solar power installation at full price or connecting to an electrical utility, the utility company still wins because a solar power system requires many years of operation before homeowners will get the full payback for investment. If homeowners considered an installation that did not make a connection to the grid, the cost would be even greater because it would require deep cycle batteries to store power for use while the sun is not shining. Typically, these batteries only last about eight years.

Net metering, which is available in the U.S., means that on-site power storage is not necessary whenever a grid connection is available, and this was one of the breakthroughs solar power needed to receive a boost in its adoption rate. As mentioned previously, net metering is a government mandate that utility companies must accept power back to the grid and give residential customers full credit for the electricity value. Effectively, the customer can generate the electricity at any opportune time, when the sun is shining or when the wind is blowing, and use the electricity whenever they want, at no additional charge. It is common to rate the price of solar power in terms of dollars spent for installation per watt produced; the average cost in 2008 was roughly $7 per peak watt installed — the cost of the bare PV modules is about $2 per watt. In addition to the solar panels, the installed price includes the cost of inverters that change the direct current from the panels into alternating current in general use. When you add in the other components, racking, and labor, this roughly doubles the cost. This equates to an approximate cost of $.20-$.35 per kilowatt hour, much more than the current price of electricity in the U.S., which, depending on area, was about $.12 per kilowatt hour at the end of 2010.

In some countries, the cost of electricity is much more, so solar can stand on its own merits; in states with good government incentives, solar already can be competitive. There is no doubt that solar cost is reducing as it is further developed, and there is little doubt that fossil fuels will become more expensive over the years, which will contribute to a gradually increasing cost for electricity from the utility company. The cost of solar has reduced by about 50 percent every ten years for the last couple of decades — it was $50 per watt in 1976 — and if this continues even without fossil fuel hikes, solar is rapidly going to be competitive in its own right. The goal for true competition would be an installed cost of $2 to $3 per watt.

With the economies of scale and a much larger production and installation network envisaged, current talk is for a goal of $1 per peak watt, and when the technology and manufacturing facilities can match this, solar likely will be installed much more widely. Apart from improving the output power for a given area, several other facets of solar PV manufacturing can be refined. The crystalline silicon used is subject to breaking, and by automating the manufacturing process made possible by much larger production, the incidence of this will be reduced. Thin-film technology, although not so efficient per unit area, also has the capability of significantly reducing the installed costs.

Going forward, there are ambitious goals for adopting solar power, and there is momentum building with the government's help. Rather than limiting the tax incentives to $2,000, since 2009 the U.S. government has allowed 30 percent against the whole cost of the installation as a federal personal tax credit — which reduces your personal tax bill — that will help in the public's acceptance.

Silicon companies

During the recent years, there has been a worldwide shortage of silicon suitable for photovoltaic use. This may seem surprising because silicon is the second most common element in the earth's crust, second only to oxygen. We learn as youngsters that sand is basically silica, and several other types of minerals can yield silicon. For some years during the infancy of solar panel manufacturing, companies could use the offcuts from semiconductor manufacturing, but by 2007, the solar industry had become the largest consumer of raw silicon. The solar industry now competes with the semiconductor industry for high-grade silicon, which is either mono- or multi-crystalline and is in comparatively short supply.

Companies involved in manufacturing and the provision of raw silicon include Hemlock Semiconductor (**www.hscpoly.com**), which is Michigan based and has Dow Corning as one of its backers. Toward the end of 2010, Hemlock announced an expansion into Clarksville, Tennessee, worth $1.2 billion, as well as a $1 billion expansion to its facility in Michigan. Other companies that are major silicon suppliers include REC Solar Grade Silicon (**www.recgroup.com/en/recgroup**) in Washington, which also produces solar modules and panels; Wacker Chemie AG (**www.wacker.com/cms/ en/home/index.jsp**), which is based in Germany but has worldwide offices and is also building in Tennessee; and Tokuyama Corporation (**www. tokuyama.co.jp/eng/index.html**) from Japan with American offices near Chicago.

Although it is the smaller companies that have been spearheading research and design into solar power and that possibly represent the most risky but potentially most profitable investments, major U.S. companies are certainly eager to take part in the market. In April 2011, 3M announced plans to build a production facility in China, its ninth in that country. This facility is centered on products to do with solar energy, unlike its previous plants, and is being built in the Hefei High-Tech Industrial Development Zone.

The most interesting renewable energy product being researched and created there is 3M™ Scotchshield™ Film, a type of film applied to the backs of conventional photovoltaic modules to protect them from contamination and moisture. At present, it is produced in Decatur, Alabama, but it seems likely that most of the production will shift to China. The film is expected to be supplied to several Chinese solar panel manufacturers, which makes the move to production there a rational one. Although 3M has been involved with renewable energy for some decades by providing films and tapes, it was in 2009 that it formed a Renewable Energy Division to concentrate on the growing market.

Non-silicon companies

Many companies are researching solar photovoltaic systems, and many different types of systems are being examined to find materials that are more efficient, more cost-effective, and/or more plentiful than silicon. In many senses, it is a race to a competitive level of pricing (about $2-$2.50 per watt installed), which would then compete directly with the fossil fuels. Companies working with non-silicon technologies include Nanosolar (**www.nanosolar.com**) with its copper indium gallium selenide (CIGS) technology, Konarka (**www.konarka.com**) using titanium dioxide, and Nanosys (**www.nanosysinc.com**), which involves re-engineering materials on a molecular level. Honda has a wholly owned subsidiary, Honda Soltec (**www.world.honda.com/group/HondaSoltec**), that currently uses CIGS to make 11.7 percent efficient panels and is looking toward improving them to 13 percent during 2011.

California-based Nanosolar in particular is positioning itself to take advantage of California's progressive laws. In 2006, Gov. Arnold Schwarzenegger signed into law the Million Solar Roofs program that aims to have solar panels on the roofs of 1 million dwellings by 2018. The output is estimated to be 3000 MW, which is equivalent to taking 1 million cars off the road in terms of carbon dioxide emissions. Two important steps toward accomplishing this goal were implemented in 2011. First, net metering was extended so utility companies would have to pay consumers for any excess electricity generated rather than just accepting electricity to offset their residential consumption. Although solar power remains somewhat expensive, this measure may work; however, when solar power becomes competitive for return on investment, homeowners can become mini generating plants and receive payment at full retail rates for excess power, which will be an untenable position for the utility companies. The second measure is that any developers building more than 50 houses must offer a solar power option to buyers. As of 2010, Nanosolar was still wrestling with production difficulties and has not achieved the target production yet, but the company remains hopeful, and if the goals are achieved, it will be very competitive.

GE also has announced its intention to build the nation's largest solar panel factory in the U.S., and it is projected to manufacture enough solar panels to power 80,000 houses annually. At the time of writing, the location of this factory is not decided, but several sites are being assessed. The technology is planned to be thin-film cadmium telluride, which the company claimed to be able to manufacture to a record 12.8-percent efficiency.

The company recently acquired PrimeStar Solar, based in Colorado, a manufacturer of thin-film solar panels, and the new factory will take advantage of their expertise. It appears to be part of a planned expansion into renewable energy following GE's massive growth in the wind turbine market in recent years.

Undoubtedly, there will be considerable growth in all types of solar products, both silicon and non-silicon based. Not all companies currently competing will survive, but the technology is getting to the state where it is becoming clearer what can be done and who is doing it. Although there is a period of great growth and even the less spectacular companies may find themselves doing good business, as an investor, you need to identify the excellent companies you can stay with. For some, the market may be a little too turbulent, and there, no doubt, will be many mergers and acquisitions in the industry that can impact investments. In the long term, the large, well-funded multinationals probably will triumph but also will have done so by incorporating smaller startup companies that are succeeding, and these will be the stellar performers of the market sector.

Solar's future

From an investor's standpoint, solar power is still sorting itself out. You can see from the range of technologies covered in this chapter that no clear winner is decided yet, and even if one seems to appear, the situation may change a year or two later. You have only to think of the VHS versus Betamax battle to realize that even with excellent engineering, there is no guarantee of success.

There are two ways you may wish to play the solar opportunity. In the long term, there will be excellent growth for the well-founded and well-funded companies. As with all investing, you should look at the quality of the management team and not be blinded by the latest science. Taking this approach, you can identify some buy-and-hold opportunities for the long term. Given the current market penetration, even if the solar industry cannot establish a major share of the utility market, this still represents a manyfold increase in the current levels.

If you are a follower of technology, you could take an alternative approach for some of your portfolio and try to stay abreast of the solar power news. This effectively would be trading the news, a short-term trading strategy where your trades are influenced by current events. Be warned that professional investors usually can act before the public on hot news, and something exceptional is usually priced in as soon as you see it. However, if you use your interest and knowledge to predict the particular technologies that may be showing promise at any particular time, that could be a reason for investment.

COMPANIES MENTIONED IN THIS CHAPTER

Citizenre (**www.citizenre.com**)

RentSolar (**www.rentsolar.com**)

RentalSolar (**www.rentalsolar.com**)

Hemlock Semiconductor (**www.hscpoly.com**)

REC Solar Grade Silicon (**www.recgroup.com/en/recgroup**)

Wacker Chemie AG (**www.wacker.com/cms/en/home/index.jsp**)

Tokuyama Corporation (**www.tokuyama.co.jp/eng/index.html**)

Nanosolar (**www.nanosolar.com**)

Konarka (**www.konarka.com**)

Nanosys (**www.nanosysinc.com**)

Honda Soltec (**www.world.honda.com/group/HondaSoltec**)

Chapter 5

Wind and Wave Power

n contrast to solar power, wind energy has been around for a long time. It often is harnessed purely as mechanical energy, for example driving windmills to grind grain or to work well pumps in remote fields, and increasingly, wind is being used to generate electricity. This is a proven and reliable power source while the wind blows, but unlike solar power, which given sunny days is generally of the same strength, the wind can vary and prove unreliable. Nonetheless, wind has been the fastest-growing source of new power generation in recent years. The following chart is compiled from data from the U.S. Department of Energy (**energy. gov**).

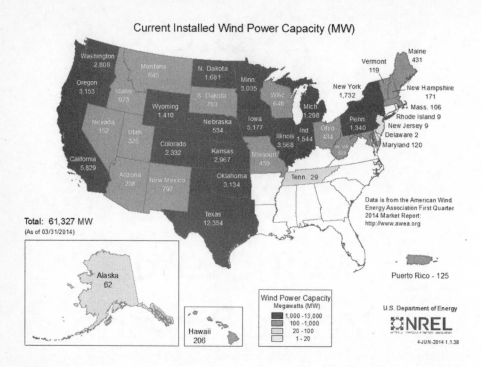

Current Installed Wind Power Capacity (MW)

Washington 2,808
Oregon 3,153
Idaho 973
Montana 645
N. Dakota 1,681
Minn. 3,035
Wyoming 1,410
S. Dakota 783
Wisc. 648
Mich. 1,298
Nevada 152
Utah 325
Colorado 2,332
Nebraska 534
Iowa 5,177
Ind. 1,544
Ohio 434
California 5,829
Arizona 238
New Mexico 797
Kansas 2,967
Oklahoma 3,134
Missouri 459
Illinois 3,568
W. Va.
Texas 12,354
Tenn. 29

Vermont 119
Maine 431
New York 1,732
New Hampshire 171
Mass. 106
Rhode Island 9
New Jersey 9
Delaware 2
Maryland 120
Penn. 1,340

Data is from the American Wind Energy Association First Quarter 2014 Market Report: http://www.awea.org

Total: 61,327 MW
(As of 03/31/2014)

Alaska 62

Hawaii 206

Puerto Rico - 125

Wind Power Capacity
Megawatts (MW)
■ 1,000 -13,000
■ 100 -1,000
□ 20 -100
□ 1 -20

U.S. Department of Energy

NREL

4-JUN-2014 1.1.38

Unlike solar power discussed in the previous chapter, wind power has been expanding steadily using tried and true technology for many years. It shares with solar power the handicap that it depends on weather for its ability to generate electricity, and this means that both technologies never can be considered the exclusive power producers no matter how large the installation without some form of electricity storage. Although impressive in its expansion, even in 2009, electric power from wind generation only amounted to 1.9 percent of the U.S. total, at 73,886 thousand megawatts. The actual installed capability is 34,296 MWh. Although considerable, as with solar power, the rate of expansion needs to be high for it to contribute any significant amount to the grid in the near future. The positive side of this otherwise gloomy outlook is that it suggests there is great scope to invest in an industry struggling to expand quickly enough to satisfy the market. One of the factors contributing to this rapid expansion is that there are both federal incentives and state renewable standards. Interest-free financing is available to government bodies that invest in wind power, and recent farm bills contain guarantees and loan provisions for rural entities that pursue wind projects. The farm bill was reauthorized in 2012 (The Food Conservation and Energy Act 2008 was its official title), and the measures last for about five years. Typically, the grants available cover up to 25 percent of the installation cost, and loan guarantees extend to 75 percent to encourage agricultural producers and small rural businesses to contribute to the country's electricity needs.

What is Wind Power?

You may have learned in the past that the sun actually causes wind. In effect, wind power is just a mechanical form of solar power. There are other influencing factors, such as mountains and valleys, the earth's rotation, bodies of water, and general weather patterns, but it is the uneven heating of the atmosphere that causes air to rise, which makes the other air come from the sides to prevent a vacuum from forming. Wind is caused by different atmospheric pressures, the highs and lows that you see on a weather chart.

Wind has been used to generate electricity for some decades and found general acceptance in the 1970s, although it would be wrong to claim that even now it has penetrated the market to any great extent. In a similar way to solar panels, a lot of the cost has to be borne up front; however, there is some maintenance required for the moving parts of a wind turbine.

Some turbines are designed to operate at a constant speed and produce the most power when facing a steady wind. Other turbines are designed to operate with a variable wind. It is important that the turbine and the site are well matched because, even in the best of times, a wind turbine will only produce 30 to 40 percent of its maximum capacity due to the varying wind conditions.

The mechanics of a wind turbine are simple in concept. On a small scale, it may be similar to a weather vane and a small airplane. The weather vane or tail allows the top of the tower to swivel, which points the propeller into the wind. The propeller spins as the wind passes over the aerodynamic blades. In the same way a propeller that an engine turns generates wind to pull an airplane through the air, the propeller the air turns produces power to turn a generator.

A small generator may be mounted at the top of the tower and driven directly. For larger wind turbines, such as those utility companies install, there is usually a system of gearing behind the propeller to drive the generator. If you have noticed these large turbines when you drive in certain states, you have seen the blades turn relatively slowly. The gears increase the rotational speed to drive a generator. Larger turbines generally cannot rely on a weather vane to point them toward the prevailing wind as it would take too much force, but they use a motorized swivel.

Turbine Location

A number of factors influence a wind turbine's location. Detailed maps are available showing the strength of wind in various areas of the country, and that is a good starting point. The U.S. Department of Energy (US DOE) has maps that can be found at **www.windpoweringamerica.gov/ windmaps**. But before locating a turbine, it is necessary to check the soil conditions to see whether such a large structure can be erected safely, to make sure that it will be easy to connect to the grid, and to deal with any neighbors' objections. It is not immediately obvious, but a wind turbine can be quite noisy and a nuisance to surrounding residents.

Some developers are looking for offshore locations to get away from problems with the residents and to benefit from the stronger, steadier wind available over the ocean. Tying the power produced on the ocean turbines back to the land can be expensive, and maintaining offshore rigs is more problematic.

Once a wind turbine is installed, the rest is easy. The well-sited turbine as a commercial investment can produce electricity at a price on par with conventional generation methods. Unlike burning conventional fuels, wind is free, and the price will never go up; so, you can expect installations to become more competitive. With the amount of engineering that has gone into developing wind turbines, the expected life is 20 to 25 years, and actual maintenance is minimal. Despite the fact that the blades are enormous, they are a long way off the ground and are not threatening to the public. And with only a tower on the ground, most of the land is available for farming uses, which makes wind power an ideal supplement to help agricultural businesses survive.

One reason for the growth in size of wind turbines is that fewer are required for a given output. Another important reason is that they become more economical as they get larger, as smaller turbines are less efficient. In fact, there are two concepts of wind turbine development: one pointing toward large wind farms to supply thousands of consumers, and another model that envisages many small wind farms, perhaps on agricultural farms, that generate power closer to the points of consumption and are less conspicuous.

In the same way as solar energy, wind power cannot provide electricity 24 hours a day and therefore, never can be considered a base generating method, that is, a generator that can always supply power when needed. By linking wind farms in different areas, the load can be smoothed out to some extent, and if combined with solar power, there is further smoothing as hot, sunny days that can be relatively calm will help solar panels create a better output. *Other methods to deal with fluctuations in electrical supply are discussed in Chapter 6, which deals with energy storage.*

The State of Development

The world's largest wind turbine is the Enercon E126, which produces about 6 MWh and is expected to increase to 7 MWh. This is enough to power 5,000 homes in Europe (Enercon is a German company), though it would power fewer than 2,000 American homes. The tower is 453 feet high, and the diameter of the rotor is 413 feet. In 2011, Norway finished a 10 MWh machine that has a 553-foot tower and floats offshore to capture higher winds.

Without doubt, there is a wind turbine shortage in the world, and the sector is booming. There are a number of incentives, not just in construction, but also from consumers choosing to pay for green power. In 2005, green wind power was cheaper than conventional electricity for a number of retail customers because of the fuel surcharge applied to conventional power. Although this changed when conventional surcharges dropped again, it indicates how close wind power is to parity with other generating systems.

Companies such as Southwest Windpower (**www.windenergy.com**) in Arizona are advocating the extreme alternative approach to wind-generated power. They are the world's largest maker of small wind systems. GE, which manufactures large wind turbines, has hedged its position by investing in them, so it appears that the future may indeed go both ways. Southwest Windpower manufactures what may be considered residential wind turbines and has sold 170,000 of them since it started in 1987. The small sector really started in the late 1990s, and now it boasts as a client George H.W. Bush, who has one for his home in Maine. Using the net metering facility with the grid-tied home, it is reported that electricity bills have been dramatically reduced, and the $17,500 typical installation cost compares favorably with installing solar panels. Interestingly, Southwest Windpower and others in the small turbine field seem to have it to themselves, as the bigger companies are pursuing commercial wind farm turbines.

CASE STUDY:
A LIFELONG PASSION

Peter Cox
Analyst
GreenTech Opportunities
Suite 1510, 800 West Pender St.
Vancouver, B.C.
Canada V6C 2V6
(604) 697-0029
or toll free (877) 773-7677
www.greentech-opportunities.com
info@greentech-opportunities.com

Born in Lyon, France, Peter's family emigrated to Vancouver, Canada, when he was a young boy. Upon graduating from the University of British Columbia in the year 2000, he moved to Germany to pursue a career in that country's emerging renewable energy industry. He began by interning with a wind farm development company in Hannover, Germany. He then completed an MBA in Energy and Environmental Management from the University of Twente in the Netherlands.

Following his degree, he remained with the local energy company (Stadtwerke Hannover in northern Germany) to continue development of his biogas thesis project. Based in part on Peter's thesis work, a biogas production and gas grid feed-in plant is now in operation on the outskirts of Hannover. His work in Germany included experience in other aspects of clean energy, such as project development and translation work with Europe's most energy efficient building standard, the Passiv Haus, and work on solar photovoltaic projects in Freiburg, Germany.

Energy production is arguably our greatest environmental and economic challenge, a reality that increasingly has forced itself onto the public consciousness over the past decade. We have experienced the ravages of fossil fuel mining and extraction, and we have to deal with the widespread negative impacts of fossil fuel burning on our natural ecosystems (land, air, and water). With the disastrous recent failure of another nuclear power plant, the massive oil spill in the summer of 2010, and rising crude oil prices, we have been forced to confront the dark side of our continued reliance on conventional sources of energy.

These environmental and economic realities are driving the search for alternatives and have already led to significant successes. After two decades of development, more than 200 gigawatts (GW) of wind turbines were in operation around the world by the end of 2010, generating roughly 440 terawatt hours (TWh) of electricity (equivalent to the electricity demands of a G7 country such as France). If the past decade's growth in wind turbine installations can be repeated in the coming decade, we should expect to see 2000 GW of wind power in operation by 2020. These wind turbines will generate more than 4000 TWh of electricity, equivalent to the electricity demands of China, now the world's largest electricity consumer (with the U.S. coming in second).

As can be seen by just this one example, the coming decade could see the most dramatic change in our energy production infrastructure that we have ever experienced. This change will be necessary if we are to confront the environmental challenges we face. Working where I do today at **Greentech Opportunities**, I am fortunate to be able to stay on the leading edge of this coming change, informing our readers ahead of the investing public. It is a fantastic time to be in this vital and growing industry.

I have had a keen interest in sustainability and clean technology since taking part in elementary school science fair projects. In other words, since

I became aware of our planet Earth. My interest waned somewhat in my late teens, but by the time I graduated with my bachelor's degree (in an unrelated field), I had decided to pursue a career in the clean-tech field. Visiting Expo 2000, the World's Fair held in Hanover, Germany, played a role in this decision. I was exposed to the exciting developments taking place in Germany and realized that here was an industry with a future. More important, here was a fledgling industry that proposed different ways of producing that key element to life on Earth: useful energy.

In my current position at GreenTech Opportunities, I inform a retail investor audience about the emerging clean energy sector on a regular basis. Clean energy spans a variety of industries and technologies, it is a vibrant and quickly changing sector, and investors are looking for guidance in order to understand it. With Wall Street being slow to discover certain clean energy sectors (due to their small initial size), we are helping investors learn about new companies before the wider investing public does so. From wind and solar energy (the two largest renewable energy industries), to geothermal and run-of-river hydro, we also cover smart grid developments and energy conservation technology.

One of the keys in my background was completing my MBA. In addition, although not an engineer, I did spend my first 18 months at the University of British Columbia (UBC) studying engineering and always have wanted to understand how things work.

At the same time, I often wondered what the wider potential of certain technologies might be. Eventually graduating from UBC with a bachelor's degree in history and political science, I have tried to understand how older energy technologies have evolved, as well as being aware of how recent energy policies have helped to advance newer ones. Lest this seem like I planned it, I have been fortunate that my first degree ended up helping me in this way.

Without wanting to sound precocious, I think humans have a responsibility for taking care of our planet Earth. Let me be clear: no matter what we as a species manage to do, the planet will eventually take care of itself. However, our existence on this planet is due to a set of incredibly unique, wonderful and, to some extent, still mysterious circumstances. For our own self-interest, we should be trying to protect these fragile circumstances.

Our current ways of generating useful energy continue to leave a terrible toll on the environment, whether our land, water, or air. One could argue that, of any industry today, the energy industry leaves the largest negative impact on our planet. According to the best of our scientific knowledge, we cannot continue on our present path.

Alternative means of generating useful energy are being developed and need to be implemented as soon as economically feasible. Informing investors about these advances is one of the keys to seeing this happen, as these are all capital-intensive industries and are in need of increased investor participation. This is even more important in the post-2008 economy, as capital for new investment purposes continues to be difficult to access.

The biggest problem I have faced in my work is the skepticism of the public toward the potential of renewable energy to supply us with 100 percent of our energy needs. Many myths are being regurgitated in the mainstream press about the supposed faults of renewable energy, which unfortunately is slowing the adoption of these new technologies. Apart from informing our readers about technological developments, much of my time is spent dispelling false arguments.

According to economists, one of the main drivers of this global recession was the huge spike in crude oil prices into the summer of 2008. To me, this event only reinforced the importance of finding alternatives to generating useful energy, adding to the many environmental reasons for pursuing this line of work. As key renewable energy technologies, such as wind and solar, continue to lower their costs and are now successfully challenging traditional fossil fuels on an economic basis (especially wind), we should see dramatic changes in our energy infrastructure in the coming decade.

A childhood interest in trying to reduce our impact on the planet was key to my starting on this path. I developed an appreciation and understanding of the basic theories of science and eventually wanted to inform myself about new technologies. Finally, I felt that the most effective way for me to contribute to the emerging clean-tech sector would be to understand the investment industry and its potential for driving real change. Writing about the clean-tech industry for a wider audience, and specifically about how to invest in it, has turned out to be an excellent opportunity for me to combine a rather diverse set of skills.

I would advise someone who was interested in doing the same to read everything you can about the industry; continue to learn; understand why certain previous technologies were not successful. Reflect on your own capabilities; consider where you might best use them; and do not hesitate to ask people in the industry for advice. With the industry being only a couple of decades old (at most), and growing so quickly, no one is really an expert on these emerging technologies. We are all learning from each other, wondering where the ride will take us.

Investing in Wind Power

In stark contrast to solar power, wind power is a well-known technology, even if advances such as using the nanotechnology research to develop better blades always are being made. However, investing in renewable resources in general has desirable tax and grant incentives, which can be checked online at the Database of State Incentives for Renewables and Efficiency website (**www.dsireusa.org**). Despite the rapid growth, the global recession of 2008 did slow down expansion, and a wind power project in the Texas panhandle that oil tycoon T. Boone Pickens was spearheading with the Mesa Power Group company was postponed in July 2009 and canceled January 2010.

One problem is that wind farms are better located in rural areas than near cities, and this makes power distribution more problematic. In spite of these issues, wind power appears to be booming in the U.S. Utility scale wind power is the green tech that is most competitive with power generated from fossil fuels or nuclear reactors, and that is why it is the domain of large global companies, at least for the mainstream turbines.

Large turbine manufacturers are spread across the world. In the U.S., General Electric, as GE Energy, plays a major role in developing large wind turbines; they supply two-thirds of the domestic market and act as the world's third largest supplier of wind turbines. But it has no monopoly on the world market, with Denmark's Vestas being the largest pure turbine maker, and Germany's Siemens also figuring as one of the giants. Slightly behind them is Spain's Gamesa, and Spain has passed Denmark to become the world's second-largest wind user, just behind Germany. It is not surprising that other countries have major turbine manufacturers considering the amount of power wind generates in places other than the U.S. Denmark currently generates about 20 percent of its power from wind, and Germany and Spain both produce more than 7 percent of their power from wind. In fact, Europe accounts for about 60 percent of the world's installed wind turbine capacity. Because of the relative lack of penetration of the American market, many European manufacturers are trying to expand into the U.S., which makes the field competitive.

What is clear is that there is a tremendous potential market for wind power in the U.S. Wind is an abundant source of energy, and there is a remarkable amount of wind available in the U.S. and offshore, with some estimates putting it as more important than all the American oil that has been discovered. At present, despite the global recession, it appears that wind power will continue to expand as quickly as new turbines can be made.

From an investing point of view, there are several choices. For large utility size turbines, the companies involved are international giants such as General Electric, Siemens (**www.siemens.com**), and Vestas (**www.vestas. com**). The operators of the wind farms can be large power companies, such as America's Florida Power & Light (FPL) (**www.fpl.com**) and Spain's Iberdrola (**www.iberdrolarenewables.us**), all the way down to individual farmers installing turbines on their lands. The third way to become involved in wind power is to research the component makers that supply the industry with the raw materials right through to the finished components. Some of these are established companies, and some are still forming and will go public in the future. Technology involved in this industry includes carbon fiber for the blades and specialized electronics for controls.

Wave Power

Wave power in some of its forms is similar to wind power, but it uses natural currents of water rather than air to generate electricity. Many wave power solutions use the motion of surface waves to generate mechanical work, which is converted into electricity, just as the name would suggest, but other methods are still in the research stages. Rather than relying only on wave movement, power also can be generated by the more consistent movement of tides, which although not generally thought of for their power are massive forces that could be captured, for example, by damming a river with tidal flows and generating by the raising and lowering of the water level.

This is not a new idea. In the 1920s and 1930s, an engineer named Dexter Cooper persisted in pushing forward his plans to use the power of the tides flowing into and out of the Bay of Fundy, which is on the Atlantic coast of Canada, just touching Maine in North America. The choice of the Bay of Fundy was obvious, as the bay has 100 billion tons of seawater flowing into and out of it with the tides twice a day. For the sake of comparison, this is more than the outflow of all the freshwater rivers in the world. The Canadian Hydrographic Service has measured the normal tidal range at nearly 56 feet.

Fort St. Anne on the Bay of Fundy in Nova Scotia

Despite such a promising environment for natural power generation, and after the expectation of $7 million in federal funding, the U.S. Government decided that the expense was too great and abandoned the project in 1936, leaving only a few dams between islands as the reminder of what might have been.

In the 1970s, Professor Stephen Salter from Scotland invented "Salter's Duck," a float designed to resemble a teardrop, which would bob on the ocean's surface and harness mechanical energy of its movement to generate power. Prototypes were tested to capture about 90 percent of the water's energy, and it was calculated that production versions could power all of Great Britain with a simple 300-mile long string of them in the North Sea.

The driving force behind its development was the oil crisis and embargo, so when this was over, the imperative to develop a commercial installation was reduced. Some say that the nodding duck was killed by a secret report in 1982, produced by the nuclear lobby and resulting in a reduction in funding for renewables in general and a bias against wind power development. Although not implemented at the moment, Salter's Duck still could be resurrected as energy concerns become more critical.

There are a few working installations at present, but there is no unified solution to harnessing power from water movement, largely because every situation is different. Despite many years of research, no large companies are involved with marketing particular technologies. One reason for this is that the open sea is a harsh environment, which demands a particular robustness of engineering for longevity. However, some companies are starting to make progress toward recognizable and practical solutions.

There are three basic methods of extracting the power from the oceans. One uses the wave motion itself, such as the bobbing duck mentioned above; another uses the up and down motion of the water to compress air or water in a vertical device, driving machinery, and the third harnesses tidal flows in a generally similar way to hydroelectric power stations, letting dammed water flow through turbines to create power.

One company that is making a name for itself is Scotland-based Pelamis Wave Power (**www.pelamiswave.com**), named after a type of sea snake. It has a snake-like floating hinged device and generates power from the relative movement of adjacent floating sections which pumps hydraulic oil to drive generators. The amount of resistance to movement between sections can be controlled which allows full advantage to be taken of light waves while allowing the system to cope with heavy seas. In May 2011, they signed an agreement for a 10-megawatt project off the Shetland Isles in Scotland.

Also Scotland based, Aquamarine Power (**www.aquamarinepower.com**) uses what it calls "oyster" technology, with the waves pushing a hinged flap backwards and forwards — which looks like an oyster opening — to pressurize water lines. The water is piped to a conventional hydroelectric turbine onshore. Thus, they are able to claim proven technology of power generation and keep most of the functioning equipment out of the water. Although the majority of their work has been around the UK, they are looking at the West Coast of the U.S. for further projects.

Given the sometimes rough sea around the British Isles, and particularly at the northern end around Scotland, it is no surprise that several companies are based there. AWS Ocean Energy (**www.awsocean.com**) is another example, with what they call the Archimedes Waveswing technology. It is in the early stages, but it expects to deliver operable wave powered machines within five years.

Another up-and-coming company, Oceanlinx Ltd (**www.oceanlinx.com**), is based in Australia and claims to have commercially viable air column designs. These have a generating turbine mounted on top, well above sea level, and the waves go up and down within a casing, pushing and pulling air through the turbine.

There are no clear leaders in the harnessing of wave/tidal energy, and some investors may prefer to wait until there are many competing installations to see whose technology will prevail in the long term and in the sometimes harsh environment. This is one of the unknowns, and at this stage, you must recognize the immaturity of most of the available systems if you are tempted to invest. There is huge potential, but you would be wise to take particular care in choosing where your money belongs.

COMPANIES MENTIONED IN THIS CHAPTER

Southwest Windpower (**www.windenergy.com**)

Siemens (**www.siemens.com**)

Vestas (**www.vestas.com**)

Florida Power & Light (FPL) (**www.fpl.com**)

Iberdrola (**www.iberdrolarenewables.us**)

Aquamarine Power (**www.aquamarinepower.com**)

AWS Ocean Energy (**www.awsocean.com**)

Oceanlinx Ltd (**www.oceanlinx.com**)

Chapter 6

Electricity

The topic of electricity usage demands its own chapter, as it will be a continued focus in years to come. There are many ways in which electricity consumption can be modified, whether it is to use less or to make sure the peaks and troughs are ironed out, which would reduce the risk of electricity cuts and brownouts and ultimately reduce the connected capacity required.

Energy Efficiency

The cleanest form of electrical energy is using less electricity. *Chapter 9 will look in detail at the work that has been done developing techniques and technology to build green buildings, a topic that is worthy of its own book. Some such books are included in the Appendix.* Although the concept of green buildings has been around for some years, it is only recently that it seems to have taken off with practical examples.

The Chinese government stated its intention in its 11th five-year plan to cut energy consumption by 20 percent. It actually achieved a 19.1 percent reduction, which is impressive considering it was developing and expanding its economy. Using energy efficiently in any country should be one of the first focuses for cutting consumption and consequently the amount spent on electricity. Even for a residential home, before installing heating and cooling equipment, attention is given to ensure the building is insulated and drafts are eliminated. This allows air-conditioning equipment to be sized appropriately to match the new need, rather than installing an oversized energy hog and perhaps looking to insulate later.

"Smart" Use

There is more to using energy efficiently than insulation. Using energy efficiently allows an overall reduction in carbon emissions and reduces the demand that in many areas, particularly fossil fuel power generation, is outpacing the increase in supply. The financial incentive is both personal and can be subsidized by government. The Federal Energy Regulatory Commission (FERC) estimates that utility companies in the U.S. could reduce peak energy demand by 7 percent, which would save $15 billion a year, by employing "smart" sensors that control when appliances are operated.

A familiar initial first step to try to reduce peak consumptions is the well-known on-peak and off-peak tariff of the utility supplier. This relies on a consumer's good sense and desire to save money to reduce peak power consumption, for example, by running a dishwasher during the cheaper night tariff. The so-called smart grid is a development of this idea and gives the utility company better control of the consumer's usage. A step toward the smart grid that is already being deployed in about 6 percent of all American homes is the smart meter, which can be read remotely. A leader in the technology, Xcel Energy, has applied this system throughout Boulder, Colorado. At its most basic, the smart grid would replace meter reading, but there are plans to do much more than that with it.

Although it has been an enormous task to supply cheap electrical power to the nation from centralized generating plants, smart grid technology is set to revolutionize the industry once again. Consider when it gets hot in August and people turn up the air conditioning while relaxing in front of their big screen TV; the utility company has to do its best to keep providing power in the worst of circumstances. At some stage, the utility may reach capacity and have to buy power from adjoining authorities. If there is no more power to be had, there may be blackouts. Even in the U.S., power outages are calculated to cost businesses at least $50 billion a year. As Americans are well served for power, in other parts of the globe outages are much more frequent.

The utility company has a difficult time dealing with this, as any new power generation takes a few years to get online. This means the utility is forced to make capital investment to expand power generation several years before it may be required. The consequences of not making the investment, if the demand does increase, would be more blackouts, brownouts, or additional expenses incurred from buying electricity from neighboring utilities. But if the investment is made and the demand is not forthcoming, it may be considered wasted expenditure. Even as it stands right now, utility companies are forced to have a peak generating capacity, which is about twice as much as is needed on an average day, just to cope with exceptional circumstances. This gives an insight into the problems a utility provider must consider in order to maintain an acceptable service. If any factor is not taken into account and it results in a failure of service for even the shortest time, it disrupts business and home users, particularly in this connected age, and leads to many complaints, so the pressure is on the utility provider to over provide as a guarantee, which is, of course, wasteful.

When you add to these concerns the fact that meter readers must physically read many thousands of meters in one service area alone, you can see that the electrical supply industry is ready for a streamlining of the process to bring it into the information age. The fundamental requirement for this is that the grid becomes a two-way communicating device so the utility company can receive information from each consumer's premises. By 2007, about 10 percent of U.S. homes were equipped with smart meters, but the predictions are that the majority of users will be connected within the next couple of years. Communication from each meter is wireless and, depending on the terrain and area, may be sent directly to the utility company's head office or may be picked up by receivers in mobile vehicles.

Once communication is established, a whole range of possibilities becomes available, limited mainly by the imagination. The first focus is on equipment such as heaters and air conditioners that are traditional power hogs. A program being used in Florida requires consumers to agree to give the utility partial control over certain appliances in return for a reduction in their bills. This system is called demand response, as the demand is reduced in response to grid loading. Although there may be some interruption to comfort levels if the air conditioning unit is turned on and off or reset in response to demand, control of other heavy loads such as water heating may not even be noticed by the consumer.

An alternative approach is to give the consumer more information and allow sticker shock, that is, a realization of the actual costs of electricity to help consumers save energy. A company called Blue Line Innovations, based in Canada and founded in 2003, sells a power monitor for around $100 that can give you information on how much your ongoing electrical usage is costing you. There are two parts to the device: a wireless transmitter that straps onto your meter and a display unit. The PowerCost Monitor™ works with Microsoft Hohm™ and with Google PowerMeter™, both systems that are designed to help keep you informed of your energy usage.

When you combine what the utility company can do with the smart meter and the effect of customers monitoring their own usage in real time, you start to get some appreciable savings. The Pacific Northwest National Laboratory (PNNL), one of the Department of Energy's National Laboratories, has calculated that using smart grid technology to rationalize loads could save from $46 billion to $117 billion in infrastructure. They are saying that $600 million of smart appliances that respond to the conditions in the overall grid could save enough capacity to avoid spending another $6 billion on generating plants. An incidental benefit of smart technology is that detailed data becomes available to the utility company that can support its planned efficiency improvements, and this translates into carbon reduction credits that can be traded on exchanges, as detailed in Chapter 12. Without this data, any savings could not be proved and, thus, are worthless.

The smart grid market used to be dominated by International Business Machines (IBM) and Echelon, which has been instrumental in developing embedded networking technology. Echelon developed LonWorks, an energy control network that makes appliances and equipment intelligent, which allows them to communicate in each direction and connects them together. For the smart grid market, LonWorks has developed the NES (Networked Energy Services) smart metering system. But with the popularity building, many other competitors have entered the market, including startups with innovative ideas. The growth prospects for smart grid are enormous, as according to current projections it only will take a few years for many of the world's power grids to be upgraded.

Lighting

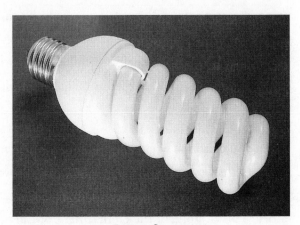

Compact fluorescent

It has been estimated that 22 percent of electrical power generated in the U.S. is used for lighting. In recent years, the energy efficient compact fluorescent light bulb (CFL) has made little headway in replacing the traditional incandescent bulbs, but this is set to change by diktat. By law (the Energy Independence and Security Act of 2007, signed into law by former President George W. Bush), most incandescent bulbs were phased out in 2014. 2011 was the cutoff for 100W bulbs; after 2012, 75W bulbs were prohibited, and a year later both 40W and 60W bulbs were as well. IKEA was the first to stop selling incandescent bulbs ahead of the deadline and now offers CFLs, LED, and halogen bulbs.

There is widespread consumer disquiet about this law, as many people believe the CFL bulbs have a light that is a different "color" or is colder than conventional bulbs, and they are not yet readily available in dimmable form. However, it is unlikely that the law will be changed to allow a prolonging of the switchover, as Europe started banning incandescent bulbs in 2010. There is the alternative of LED light bulbs, but these are even more expensive than CFLs. CFL bulbs are currently about $3 to $4 each, but LED bulbs range from $10 to $25. CFL bulbs also have a useful life of 6,000 to 10,000 hours, and LED bulbs last 40,000 to 60,000 hours. The cost gain is that for the same light output, the new alternatives offer a greatly reduced energy use when compared to incandescent.

A few decorative bulbs are exempt from the ban — three-way bulbs, appliance bulbs, and plant lights — and because the rest of the world is already a step ahead in mandating the changeover, it will not be possible to go across the border to Canada to stock up on the older bulbs, as they already will have switched. That is not to say that all is going to be perfect with the changeover because if a CFL bulb breaks, a small amount of mercury is released. Another alternative, the electron stimulated luminescence (ESL) bulb, contains no toxins, and though it is more expensive than a CFL bulb, it is cheaper than LED. There is still a possibility that an alternate technology may be developed that receives better consumer acceptance.

Apart from that distant opportunity, many CFL bulbs are made in China, and it is an established technology. There may be some developments in terms of changing the perceived "color" of the lamps that you can find with fluorescent tubes now, picking "warm white" or "daylight" hues for example. But investing in light bulb manufacturers would require following general investing guidelines, rather than looking for a boost for clean-tech reasons, as the market and manufacturing are in place.

Energy Storage

One problem referred to in the previous chapter regarding solar and wind power generation is that of providing a continuous power supply that responds to the consumers' demands. Both solar photovoltaic and wind power are subject to the vagaries of the weather and need to be supplemented by an alternate electricity source to meet the needs of the grid. Truly, the large-scale adoption of solar and wind power can be a problem to the electrical utility company, which has to be able to meet peak demand regardless of whether the sun is shining or the wind is blowing and therefore, must install generating capacity to deal with the peak.

In itself, consumers adding surplus solar- and wind-produced electricity to the grid do little to help the utility company save on generating equipment investment. In fact, if consumers add the power through net metering, which rebates the customers for the energy given back, the utility company has a reduced income while still needing to make the same capital investment. The utility company would save the amount of fossil fuel that was previously used to create the power that is received, and that would be less than the credit it is mandated to give. To help alleviate these problems and provide a means of dealing more effectively with peak loads so the online generating capacity is not overtaxed during peak periods, electric companies increasingly will need to develop the means to store power,

One familiar method of storing power is the provision of batteries. There is no doubt that battery developments will continue, and this field will continue to expand. *This is discussed in more detail in Chapter 10 on transportation, as it is such an inherent part of the development of plug-in hybrids and electric vehicles.* The current chapter talks about stationary energy storage, such as the type of storage that can be used to store power from photovoltaic units.

As mentioned in the solar chapter, solar and wind power actually contribute little to the amount of electricity used in the U.S. This means that the potential problem for the utility companies mentioned above has not yet surfaced. However, if clean energy generated by techniques such as these is to make a real difference and become a significant part of the national power use, the energy storage problem must be addressed and solved to avoid wasted investment in conventional generation equipment.

Energy storage is an exciting new field because it has not been needed for fossil fuel-generating installations. The industry jargon identifies the power that is always available as "baseline power" — as this always must be available, however it is produced — and the power from sources such as solar and wind is referred to as a secondary source that can be added into the grid to supplement the base. As more intermittent generation plugs into the grid, the baseline generation output can be reduced to take advantage of the clean energy, but it always must be available to guarantee that the supply can be maintained.

With a suitable form of stationary storage, it is possible realistically to reduce the baseline capacity of conventional generating stations, and this will allow real savings in equipment installation. The cost of online stationary storage must be compared to this, and it has to be cheaper than building more generating stations to be viable. An example of energy storage is an off-the-grid house where there is no possibility of net metering because there is no connection to the national electrical grid. You can find examples of these in remote areas, such as cabins built far into the mountains for seclusion and privacy. Power from solar and wind generation generally is different from the power the grid supplies, as it is a direct current at the wrong voltage. The utility service is alternating current (AC). To connect to the grid, the direct current electricity has to feed into a DC to AC inverter that also includes an electronic controller to ensure the power is synchronized with the mains.

With an off-the-grid house, the solar and wind power feeds first into a charge controller that supplies direct current to a bank of batteries. The power from the bank of batteries then is used to source the inverter. As long as there is charge in the batteries, the inverter will be supplied, and the house will have power, regardless of whether the sun is shining or the wind is blowing. If not connected to the grid, the inverter works on its own with no synchronization required.

Until recent clean energy initiatives highlighted the need for more effective storage, the only commercially available form of storage was a similar system with a room full of lead acid batteries similar to those used in automobiles but designed and rated for continual charging and discharging. These batteries are called deep-cycle batteries. They are more expensive than auto batteries and require ongoing maintenance, which means they are not going to provide a practical solution for large-scale energy storage.

Fuel cells

One possible answer for storage on a commercial level is using fuel cells. Fuel cells are based on hydrogen and have been researched for vehicle use. However, the problems associated with storing hydrogen at high pressures and the lack of distribution of hydrogen at filling stations mean that fuel cells have taken a backseat as far as clean vehicles are concerned, though they still are being developed. This does not mean technology is not available and perhaps applicable to stationary applications, and the prospects are good given their efficiency.

Interestingly, fuel cells are two or three times more efficient than the typical internal combustion engine installed in a car. In a fuel cell, hydrogen is exposed to a catalyst, usually platinum, that works to produce a reaction that splits the hydrogen into its constituent parts of protons and electrons. A membrane that blocks electrons allows the protons to combine with oxygen and produce water, but the electrons must travel through wiring outside the cell, which produces electricity. This can be used to drive a motor for power generation.

Flow batteries

You are no doubt familiar with most forms of traditional batteries. Appliance batteries, such as the kind you buy in a grocery store, come in several standard sizes and are available in rechargeable form. Lead acid batteries, typically found in automobiles, have different capacities, are rechargeable, and are all of a similar configuration. What these batteries have in common is that they are a fixed size and have a certain amount of chemical electrolyte, the active ingredient that generates electricity.

One of the dark horses on the clean energy front is the flow battery. Really only suitable for stationary operation, the flow battery has a central battery unit but has external tanks filled with electrolyte. The electrolyte is pumped

through the battery as needed, which is where the name "flow battery" is derived. Whenever the battery power starts to weaken, more electrolyte can be circulated. The larger the external tanks, the more electricity the battery can store. Recharging can be as simple as refilling the tanks with fresh electrolyte. A few companies are heavily involved with developing flow batteries, and the word is that this technology may provide a competitively priced means of storage, with an equipment cost below $100 per kilowatt-hr. For comparison, lithium ion batteries cost about $500 to $1,000 per kWh.

Three companies are currently worth watching in this field, which is still very much in the experimental stage. Deeya Energy (**www.deeyaenergy. com**), based in California, continues to attract venture capital and has the distinction of employing flow battery inventor Lawrence Thaller.

The company was founded in 2004 and is building a viable product in India. A small young company called EnerVault (**www.enervault.com**), also based in California, is looking to create some competition to Deeya, but both these companies may be outflanked by Prudent Energy (**www. pdenergy.com**), which is based in Beijing and can take advantage of lower manufacturing costs. Its batteries were designed in Canada by VRB Power, Inc., a company Prudent acquired in 2009. Other companies that may be worth looking at include EEStor, A123 Systems, and Altairnano, all of them start-ups in the race to commercial success.

Flywheels

Moving away from the chemical technologies, it also is possible to store power in flywheels, which are similar to gyroscopes. Unlike the flywheel linked to an internal combustion motor, whose purpose is principally to smooth out the unevenness of the cycle, a flywheel used for energy storage sits on a very low friction mount and stores kinetic energy, that is moving energy, by spinning. The perfect solution is that there is no friction and that any energy put into getting the flywheel moving is available for later use, which slows the flywheel down. In theory, the flywheel is a great solution for energy storage as it is long lasting and nonpolluting. In practice, many large flywheels are required to store a significant amount of power. The current state of technology is that flywheels spin in a vacuum to eliminate air friction and even use magnetic levitation to eliminate friction from bearings. There also are prototypes using high-temperature superconductor bearings.

The current state of the market for flywheel storage is that Massachusetts-based Beacon Power (**www.beaconpower.com**) is a recognized leader but has had some trouble meeting NASDAQ filing regulations; it sometimes performs as a sub-$1 stock for some periods and consequently, has been threatened with delisting. It tackled this issue by doing a reverse stock split, issuing one share for every 10 held, but still is in a precarious position. In 2011, a 20-megawatt electricity storage installation for New York began operating, which uses 200 flywheels to achieve the capacity. Revenues and cash have been declining, and the future of the company may hinge on proving its equipment to the market and investors using this installation as a case study.

In May 2011, the company announced a collaboration with Gaelectric, a wind developer in Ireland, and this gives Gaelectric marketing rights in Ireland and the United Kingdom. Gaelectric is one of the largest wind developers in Montana, and Beacon is installing a 1-MW storage system there. Despite the bright outlook, which is conveyed by these developments, Beacon Power shares (BCON) have declined consistently over several years, albeit with noticeably more interest and volume of trading during recent years.

Compressed air storage

This type of energy storage is not as widely usable as other forms of storage. There are two operational plants, one of them in Alabama and one in Germany. Two more are due to come online in the U.S. in the near future, located in Iowa and in Texas. What is required is that the intermittent power generation is located near an underground cavern or mine. This means any excess energy can be used to run a compressor that pumps air into the cavern. During peak times, the compressed air from the cavern can be released to generate electricity, perhaps by driving a turbine.

Although this sounds like a rather limited opportunity, the Electric Power Research Institute has stated it believes more than 85 percent of the U.S. has access to underground facilities that could allow compressed air storage. The great advantage of compressed air storage is there is no pollution and not much equipment needed. The amount of storage would be limited by the size of the cavern, but the facility planned for Iowa has a tentative capacity of 20 weeks worth of air.

Hydroelectric storage

Hydroelectric storage uses a proven technology that has been exploited for decades. Hydroelectric generating plants have captured the energy of water traveling from a higher reservoir to a lower reservoir and typically are located inside a concrete dam structure. The additional features to make a hydroelectric generating installation into hydroelectric storage are pumps to move water from the lower level to the upper level when there is excess power, which would provide more stored volume of water to fall through the turbines and generate electricity when required.

An alternative version of this is planned for offshore wind farms. A Dutch consultancy has put forward a plan to build a stored facility in the North Sea that would contain a reservoir space beneath the surface. In this case, the operation would allow seawater to flood the reservoir and generate electricity during the peak times. They would use surplus capacity to pump the water out at other times.

COMPANIES MENTIONED IN THIS CHAPTER

Deeya Energy (**www.deeyaenergy.com**)
EnerVault (**www.enervault.com**)
Prudent Energy (**www.pdenergy.com**)
Beacon Power (**www.beaconpower.com**)

Chapter 7

Geothermal

lthough solar and wind power have been expanding rapidly, geothermal has been sitting on the sidelines, with a 3 percent annual increase in total generation in the last decade. However, the current clean energy emphasis is causing this sleeping giant to awaken. Geothermal energy comes from the heat in the earth's core, which you can see in a dramatic form when a volcano erupts. Generally, you need to drill down to the level of the heat in order to capture and make use of this form of energy. In some areas, geothermal energy can be found in hot water underground, and in other regions, the heat must be harnessed in another way in order to provide energy. In 2008, Congress enacted a tax credit for geothermal energy. The total generation from geothermal in 2009 is given as just more than 15,000,000 MWh, much more than solar but lagging behind the generation from some other green sources such as wood products and biomass.

The curious thing about geothermal is that it crops up where you may least expect it. For example, Icelanders use a great deal of geothermal energy to warm their homes and generate electricity. Geothermal supplies 25 percent of the country's electricity, with the rest being generated by hydropower. Many buildings are heated by geothermal energy, and it is used to warm many sidewalks in Reykjavík, which helps them deal with the snow and ice problem. Add to this the advantage that geothermal is extremely clean and nonpolluting, and you might wonder why more attention has not been given to this method of extracting energy from the environment. In fact, Iceland has so much surplus heat that local companies are now using it to refine aluminum from imported bauxite, which is an energy intensive application. There are also plans to use the geothermally generated electricity

Steam rising from a geyser in New Zealand

to separate hydrogen and run fuel cells for cars and fishing boats. If this happens, Iceland will be the first country to be powered completely by renewable energy.

The U.S. Geological Survey has reported that 9 gigawatts of electricity can be generated by currently identified systems and a projected 30 gigawatts from as yet undiscovered sources.

The potential is considered enormous, but because of its nature, it is largely unseen and unknown. Some estimate that the energy contained in the layer 10,000-feet to 30,000-feet deep, which represents the limit of current drilling technology, could supply the current annual energy requirement of the U.S. for 125,000 years. Although this would be far beyond the scope of reality, it suggests that tapping into just a small amount of the energy source could make a big difference to how this energy resource is viewed.

Evidence of the potential of geothermal is plain when you consider the number of hot springs and geysers present. These are geothermal instances that generally have not required extreme measures to tap further into the resource. Far from having to drill to a minimum of 10,000 feet depth, geysers have shown themselves simply by the pressure from underground.

Unlike some energy production, no fossil fuel is required to access this source. In addition, geothermal is available 24 hours a day with no intermittency, other than plant maintenance. Noxious fumes or emissions are minimal — there may be some release from water or other material brought up from the depths, but the process usually aims to return the depleted heat source into the ground.

The starting point for understanding geothermal energy is to realize that the earth contains a vast store of heat, perhaps up to 12,632 degrees Fahrenheit. As you can see from volcanoes, the temperatures inside the earth are enough to melt rock. We live on a solid crust formed from the cooling rock. What this means is that, in general terms, the farther down you go inside the earth, the hotter it gets. The crust contains this most of the time, with outbursts as volcanoes and geysers such as Old Faithful in Yellowstone Park. If the water does not come all the way to the surface but instead is trapped by an impervious layer of rock, it can form a geothermal reservoir with pent-up energy of hot water or steam waiting to be drilled into.

Using the Energy

The easiest way of using geothermal energy is to find a source of underground steam that can drive a turbine directly. Although underground heat is the guaranteed factor, steam is harder to find, so this method of using geothermal energy is not reliable in many circumstances. Most underground reservoirs have hot water rather than steam, though when the pressure is relieved as the water comes to the surface, often that water will "flash" into steam. Water boils at a lower temperature when the pressure is low. If the steam is vented to the atmosphere, a small amount of the natural pollutants hydrogen sulfide and nitric oxide are released, but this is insignificant compared to the pollution of conventional combustion.

The common way of harvesting the underground heat to generate power is to pump water into cracks in the rocks and produce steam that can be used to drive turbines. The condensed steam that has served its purpose can be returned into the ground as water in order to keep a balance. Another method is to bring to the surface hot water that, through a heat exchanger, vaporizes a working fluid that can drive a turbine. This is called a binary cycle. The working fluid is in a closed loop, and the used hot water is piped back underground. This method has become more desirable because the water from underground is never exposed to the atmosphere, which prevents the pollution mentioned above and also obviates any risk of polluting the groundwater, at least while the plant works as designed. The working fluid used may be isobutane and is selected to work with the temperatures available.

The great thing about this method of extracting energy from geothermal sources is that the temperature can be lower, and that allows geothermal to be considered in areas where the heat is not sufficient to produce steam. This type of geothermal plant is manufactured by United Technologies and is similar to air-conditioning equipment working in reverse. Rather than an air-conditioning compressor being powered to create cooling, in this form, a turbine uses heat to create power.

United Technologies (**www.utc.com**) has developed various chemicals to work with different temperature ranges. Previously, when a test showed the available temperatures were less than 250 degrees F, there was no hope of using steam, and the potential geothermal site would be abandoned. As this binary cycle has developed, the old test wells that were considered too cool can be reopened and perhaps used. The world's lowest temperature geothermal resource is in Alaska; the plant uses this technology to generate power from 165 degree F water. Previously, Chena Hot Springs Resort used diesel to generate power as it is many miles away from the electrical grid, but now a geothermal plant from United Technologies meets the needs.

Another form of geothermal energy, though not strictly taking energy from the ground, the geothermal heat pump uses the ground as a constant temperature source from which building heat pumps can heat or cool. In this case, pipes are only sunk a few feet into the ground where the temperature is a consistent 45 F to 75 F. You may have noticed this effect from the constant temperature you find in a basement. The heat pump is similar to an air conditioning unit in that it uses a compressor to heat or cool, with the geothermal installation acting as a heat sink to conduct away heat to be rejected or to provide heat to be absorbed. This does not use the geothermal heat that is deeper underground but is a more efficient system than conventional air conditioning.

Finally, there is a method to extract heat from underground even when there is no water present. This is called an enhanced geothermal system (EGS), and it involves drilling down to the hot rocks and injecting water to be heated and produce steam. In effect, it is creating a conventional geothermal system in which there is no moisture. There are a number of variations on this, with steam rising in another shaft or through existing fractures, and sometimes impervious rock layers will block the steam, but all these engineering challenges can be addressed.

Geothermal Disadvantages

The fact that you do not pay directly for the energy as power is generated makes the economics of geothermal power similar to solar and wind. There is a large up-front cost, and in the case of geothermal, it is usually greater than for those other alternatives. This disadvantage has made adopting geothermal energy rather slow until now when there is an increased emphasis on clean power.

Geothermal power has several other issues. The first one is that there is an initial capital investment to explore the possibility of using geothermal power at any particular location. Although geologists are able to suggest possible regions, until the holes are drilled, there is no way of telling how extensive or intense the heat may be. Venture capital must support the drilling of trial wells to find out if geothermal energy is usable. These wells are not the relatively cheap drillings such as those used for consumption water. Because of the depth and complication, the trial wells may cost several million dollars, and this must be funded based on geology and expert advice, with no assurance that a viable source will be found.

Second, until the trial is done, there is no clear way of knowing how large a source is available, and how it may be used. Frederick Henderson III, a geothermal entrepreneur in Colorado, has confirmed that with conventional geothermal systems, there is no way the actual surface disturbance and size of buildings for the generating equipment can be predicted before the trial wells have been dug and the results analyzed.

Third, there is often opposition from local neighbors. Despite the fact that the power comes from underground, there is some surface disturbance and equipment required, and without the facility to predict in advance how large an installation will be needed, the fear of the unknown is likely to bring out strong opposition. If the proposed geothermal installation is in an outlying area where residents rely on wells for their water, it is difficult to assuage the concerns that their water supply may be contaminated or compromised in other ways. Indeed, in some areas the residents use the water to heat their houses and to supply hot water to swimming pools. Although they might tolerate other residential development, the idea that heat would be used commercially brings the fear that they might find themselves without sufficient heat for their own purposes.

A Texas company called Power Tube, Inc., (**www.powertubeinc.com**) has developed and patented a system that may offset many of residents' concerns. The system has been through U.S. Air Force testing for many years and is becoming ready for commercial application. It is a sealed system that extracts only the heat from underground and does not use any water or steam. Power Tube has invented the word "geomagmatic" to distinguish this technology from geothermal. The word comes from the idea of it being powered by a recharging magma, literally molten rock, heat source and distinguishes it from conventional geothermal power. Power Tube is at pains to distinguish its process from regular geothermal because, as they have pointed out, conventional geothermal energy generally is defined as using water or steam heated from the earth to drive a turbine either directly or indirectly, which the process clearly does not do. The Power Tube works with the relatively low temperature range of 230 F to 390 F, and most of the equipment is contained within the drilling shaft.

The actual equipment, from bottom to top, consists of a thermal riser to bring up heat from the depths of the earth, a heat exchanger, a turbo generator, and a three-stage condenser. The thermal riser consists of two concentric tubes that flow a fluid down to the hotter region and return it back to the equipment by natural convection. The heat exchanger is served by the hot fluid from below and vaporizes a working fluid, an isopentane/isobutane mixture, to drive the turbine. The rest of the installation below the ground is a tubular condenser that condenses the working fluid by cooling with air entrained from the surface. It is hoped that commercial tests took place in Colorado in 2011, but as of August, they still were waiting to hear about a grant to facilitate the installation.

Investing in Geothermal

Geothermal is not expected to expand rapidly. Despite its obvious advantages, there are hurdles to be overcome, particularly with respect to location and public opposition. Some people also are concerned about the possibility of triggering earthquakes by prolonged use of underground heat. This may be particularly a problem with the enhanced geothermal where water is injected and could cause cracking. Given the advantages of geothermal, you can expect a steady expansion as sites are identified and planning permission is received.

An intrinsic problem is that initial work must be done before you know if there are to be any returns. Even when a viable geothermal source is found, there is a high upfront capital investment and a waiting period before any gains are seen, and this will limit the number of projects taken on. Geothermal probably will continue to expand underneath the radar and provide opportunities for astute investors. Apart from United Technologies and Power Tube, the former with fingers in a lot of pies and the latter banking everything on geothermal, you also can consider Ormat Technologies, Inc., (**www.ormat.com**) a Nevada-based company specializing in geothermal and recovered energy and with a long background of experience in the field. Ormat builds and operates geothermal plants; it sells the resulting electricity to utilities. Calpine (**www.calpine.com**) operates similarly and is the largest independent power producer in the U.S. that also includes gas-fired power plants.

COMPANIES MENTIONED IN THIS CHAPTER

Deeya Energy (**www.deeyaenergy.com**)

EnerVault (**www.enervault.com**)

Prudent Energy (**www.pdenergy.com**)

Beacon Power (**www.beaconpower.com**)

United Technologies (**www.utc.com**)

Power Tube, Inc. (**www.powertubeinc.com**)

Ormat Technologies, Inc. (**www.ormat.com**)

Calpine (**www.calpine.com**)

Chapter 8

Water

ater is becoming a serious issue for the global community. More so than energy shortages, water shortages are difficult to deal with. If people do not have clean drinking water, disease, and death are not far away, whereas energy shortages usually can be endured with some discomfort. Seventy percent of the Earth's surface is covered by water, which leads to complacency when matters of a shortage are talked about. But it takes little more than a passing familiarity with the problem to realize that sources of fresh clean water are dwindling. Most of the Earth is covered with saltwater, which is not suitable for drinking and is of little use for irrigation. Much of the world's freshwater is locked up in the polar ice caps, though these are vanishing with the climate changes. The remainder of freshwater is in lakes and rivers that rely on replenishment by rain and ice melt. These have been put to increasing use during the 20th century when the world population tripled.

Because of its apparent abundance, in the past little thought was given to water conservation. However, with the strain that is now being placed on

the world resources, urgent attention is needed to conserve and to develop new sources of clean water. Just as with energy, conservation should be a starting point for ensuring an adequate supply of water. Conservation goes way beyond the familiar advice to turn off running water when brushing teeth or using showers rather than baths. Although these habits can help, the amount of water each American uses is far greater than the amount that comes out of the faucet. The U.S. Geological Survey (USGS) publishes figures that show 410 billion gallons of water were used per day in the United States. This is an average of more than 1,300 gallons per person of the population. Until you realize how much water is used for different applications, this figure seems unbelievable. Perhaps the only reason the average American is not aware of it is that the U.S. is rich enough to be able to engineer a way around most of the problems.

The largest uses of water include irrigation and thermoelectric power generation. An average golf course uses 684,000 gallons of water per acre every year just to keep the grass green for our pleasure. A typical American family uses more than 22,000 gallons of water every year to keep their lawn green. The largest consumption was for thermoelectric power generation, which took more than 40 percent of the freshwater usage, more than 200 billion gallons of water a day. But more than 60 million acres are now under irrigation, which accounted for 128 billion gallons of water per day in 2005. This is not to imply that all such water is for recreation and leisure, as may be thought by the examples in the paragraph above. A great deal of irrigation is for agricultural products that require massive amounts of water. Wheat is produced at the rate of 600 million tons per year globally, and each ton requires on average nearly 50,000 cubic feet of water, which is more than 350,000 U.S. gallons. Even so, it requires far more water to produce animal protein than it does to grow vegetables — a pound of potatoes requires 12 gallons of water, and a pound of beef requires more than 1,500 gallons of water.

One of the problems is that the world population is seeking a better lifestyle. China is doubling its demand for meat every ten years. India doubled its demand for poultry in five years. But before we start blaming the developing world for the situation, we must realize they still consume far less meat per capita than the U.S. population. As incomes increase, people are demanding more animal protein, and raising more animals requires more pasture land and more animal feed. Anyone who has visited Texas recently and seen the Rio Grande may be wondering why it was called that, as it appears in some areas to simply trickle. The fact is that it has been disappearing for at least 50 years, as it has been used increasingly to irrigate farms in this hot region.

The problems do not cease with current production because the world population, which is predicted to increase by 50 percent in the next 50 years, will place even greater strains on the water system as well as other resources. Already one out of six people in the world lacks access to safe drinking water. And all these listed problems are to say nothing of what happens to the rest of the natural world and the animal kingdom as natural water supplies are depleted. That can be the subject of another debate.

All these factors should indicate to you that there is a massive problem with water, and this may equate to great opportunities in environmental investing. Our naturally occurring freshwater resources are limited and need to be conserved as far as possible, but the solution also will require finding or generating a larger supply.

Natural Water Supplies

Apart from surface water, many people derive their drinking supplies from wells, and that is the source for most water companies. The underground Ogallala Aquifer, also known as the High Plains Aquifer, supplies a great deal of the U.S. water supply. It is estimated to cover 174,000 square miles, and it spreads across eight states, from Texas to South Dakota. The Ogallala Aquifer was formed about 10 million years ago and varies in depth across the vast area it covers. Water can be found at 100 feet deep in some areas, and in others is as much as 400 feet deep. The maximum depth of the aquifer is about 1,000 feet. The aquifer supplies drinking water to an estimated 82 percent of the people who live above it. Figures from the USGS suggest about 30 percent of the groundwater used for irrigation in the U.S. is derived from this aquifer.

The aquifer is recharged with rainfall and snowmelt, and over the years, this has proved woefully inadequate to maintain levels. In some places, the water level has gone down 100 feet, and some experts believe it will be depleted within 25 years. You can expect that the wealth of the U.S. will be applied in developing technology to obtain water from other sources and prevent the otherwise inevitable drought, but this gives an indication of the profligacy with which we use water.

Another source of water in the U.S. is the Colorado River. Much of the American West depends on this, which comes from the snow melting off the Rockies. It feeds into Arizona, Nevada, and Southern California, all arid areas, and, in particular, the massive expansions of Las Vegas and Phoenix in the middle of the desert have depended on it. Las Vegas is fed from Lake Mead, which in turn depends on the Colorado River. Experts suggest that with climate warming, snowmelt may half by 2050.

Even in the U.S., natural water supplies literally are drying up. The story is much bleaker in many developing countries, and there are reports from many regions of the Earth of drought and consequent famine. Although disconnected from the strife, even in the U.S., it is impossible to be unaware of the situations in India, Africa, China, and South America.

Desalination

If the available freshwater supplies cannot cope, it is natural to wonder if desalination, or taking the salt out of the water supply, may provide the answer. The oceans appear virtually limitless if freshwater can be derived from them. Certainly, for many years it has been possible technically, though a little expensive, to extract freshwater from the sea. With the increasing difficulty associated with using natural supplies due to depletion, there will be a growing cost of water, and this may result in desalination becoming more competitive.

There are two basic forms of desalination: evaporation or boiling the seawater into a vapor, and reverse osmosis, which is like filtering on a molecular level. There are many variations, particularly for the evaporative answer, and these vary in complexity and in energy needed, which is an important factor if you are considering a technology that can be applied in Third World countries. Perhaps the simplest form of the evaporative solution is to use sunlight to evaporate or boil off the water. This leaves the salt and other impurities behind. This solution, as with any other that evaporates the water, requires that the water vapor or steam be condensed on a colder surface from which it can be collected as freshwater. Sometimes this has been done with a solar still, which used to be popular but fell into disuse when water became readily available. A solar still uses the heat of the sun to evaporate water that subsequently is condensed on a sheet of glass or clear plastic and then collected. It has no moving parts and requires no power. This system also is being used in North Africa for solar thermal plants erected to provide power, to have the waste steam used to boil and desalinate seawater. If freshwater can be generated as a byproduct of another necessary process, this reduces the cost and equipment needs.

From elementary science, you may remember that the boiling point of water reduces as pressure is reduced. The typical example given is trying to brew a cup of tea on a mountaintop, where the reduced boiling point makes it difficult to have a high enough temperature for a good infusion. This can be used for desalination, with the pressure of the atmosphere over seawater being reduced until water evaporates. Again, it must be condensed and collected to supply freshwater. This form of desalination is called vacuum distillation.

As you might expect, vacuum distillation has a greater requirement for energy, so it probably is best used where there is already an available source of waste heat, such as from a power plant. Often, the water will be evaporated in stages by passing water from chamber to chamber, each at a lower pressure, and the water "flashes" into steam when the pressure is reduced. In each chamber, more of the water becomes steam and can be captured. This process is called multistage flash distillation.

The alternative to evaporative desalination, as mentioned above, is a kind of molecular filtering process called reverse osmosis, or RO. Domestic water treatment companies sometimes use this science to treat household water, and it is possible to get RO systems that install under a sink. The process requires a semipermeable hydrophilic membrane, which is the "filter." Seawater under pressure is introduced on one side of the membrane, and freshwater passes through the membrane. It is called reverse osmosis because it is the opposite of what scientists call osmosis, a process by which dissolved salts on one side of the membrane tend to equalize in concentration on both sides, a kind of natural diffusion. An example of desalination by reverse osmosis system in construction is the Carlsbad Desalination Project being erected in San Diego County in California and built by Poseidon Resources. This was approved in November 2007 but had a series of legal challenges, which delayed it until 2011. It became operational in 2013 and produces 50 million gallons of drinking water a day, which provides the county with about 10 percent of its total water supply. It provides water to about 300,000 San Diego residents.

Around the world, many thousands of working desalination plants are producing billions of gallons of water. The majority of them are in the Middle East because of the climate and because energy is cheap. However, the U.S. does have about one-sixth of the world's desalination plants, and many more are in the planning stages for California.

Desalination technology

Apart from the well-known and established systems of distillation and of reverse osmosis, research is taking place to develop more efficient methods to make seawater drinkable. Not surprisingly, these are on the "nano" level, an increasingly popular area of research. Strictly speaking, the prefix "nano" is used in the metric "Système International" (SI) system of measurement to denote a one-billionth part. For example, a nanosecond is one-billionth of a second. The term "nano" generally has been adopted to refer to technology that researches the properties of extremely small particles. One of the technologies has been nicknamed nanotube membranes and is a development of the idea from the RO systems currently being used. The process uses a membrane of carbon nanotubes that act as pores and restrict the flow to anything larger than six molecules wide. Although this works in a similar way to RO, the great advantage is that it is not so restrictive to the flow, and thus less energy is required to extract the same volume of water. In other words, freshwater, up to four times as much, can be generated for the same power. The same technology is being researched for gas purification.

Not to be confused with the above, researchers also have developed nano-composite membranes that are said to attract water ions and repel others, with the same advantage of reduced resistance. In this case, the membranes halve the energy required. This expertise has been applied to gas separations, and development has continued for several years. Both these nano-technologies are in the research stage with no practical applications now, but they are proven technologies.

Water Management

Apart from producing more water, the problem of inadequate water supplies can be tackled, as with the energy market, by managing consumption. The major uses of water are not necessarily domestic, as noted above with the vast amounts that are needed for agriculture, but saving water on all fronts benefits the overall goals.

In many countries, the underground water pipes are getting old and are suspected to be leaking. Many years of treating water as cheap and abundant has created a society in which wasting water was not considered an issue. It is obviously difficult to put a figure on this, but a report by the European Commission in 2007 thought that at least 20 percent of all water used was wasted. As with electricity, this has led to the idea of smart metering, a system to monitor water use and provide feedback to the local water utilities and/or the consumer. When the feedback is directed to the utility company, it can use this to impose restrictions on usage, such as banning irrigation during periods of drought.

However, unlike smart metering of electricity, smart water metering appears to be slow to catch on. Undoubtedly there are great benefits for the water utility company in being able to see where water is used and monitor for leakage, but according to a study commissioned by software company Oracle˚ (**www.oracle.com**), 64 percent of the water districts surveyed in the U.S. and Canada have no plans to supply smart meters in the near future. Oracle provides software to utility companies and commissioned the survey to assess the potential market.

Aside from water management to control consumption, another area of the market that is seeing expansion is water reuse. This is not the common idea of draining "greywater," water recycled from washing dishes, clothes, and from bathing, onto a garden for irrigation, but instead includes recovering and treating toilet waste, which is called "blackwater." Put more simply, it is extracting drinking water from wastewater, or sewage. The topic does not immediately generate enthusiasm because of the connotations of wastewater, but it is being applied in many areas of the world. For instance, Singapore, China, Dubai, and India use large systems provided by Hyflux (**www.hyflux.com**), a leading provider of water management and environmental solutions headquartered in Singapore, and the systems use filtration, reverse osmosis, and other processes so they can extract drinking water from wastewater. Singapore is looking for about 2 ½ percent of its freshwater to come from reuse water this year.

Another way in which wastewater is being reused, this time in the U.S., is discharging reclaimed water into underground aquifers and surface reservoirs, and this is called indirect potable reuse. The water from aquifers and reservoirs usually is treated before delivery to the public, so there is a further measure of disconnection from sewage. This system is in place in both California and Washington, D.C. Before you decide that this is taking things too far, consider that settlers historically used wells for freshwater and septic tanks or lagoons for waste and that natural filtration through the soil was the only purifier of the supplies.

Another aspect of water management is leak detection. This has been implemented by the Las Vegas Valley Water District, which has more than 8,000 leakage sensors in use and estimates that it saved more than a half billion gallons of water in two years. Fluid Conservation Systems supplied their system, and there are others in the business.

CASE STUDY: ENGINEERING ANALYSIS

Edward Guinness
Fund manager
Guinness Atkinson
Asset Management, Inc.
21550 Oxnard Street, Suite 850
Woodland Hills, CA 91367
800-915-6566
www.gafunds.com
info@aafunds.com

Edward Guinness is a fund manager at Guinness Atkinson Asset Management. Edward's management efforts focus on the solar, wind, hydro, geothermal, and biomass sectors. Guinness Atkinson's fund management team is based in London.

As fund manager for the alternative energy sector, my role can be divided into two main areas. First, I analyze the alternative energy industry and look at trends to try to identify areas of the alternative energy sector that are most attractive to invest in.

Second, I analyze specific companies that we are invested in or that we are interested in investing in. These are thrown up both by our sector research and by a screening tool we use to identify companies that fit with the Guinness Atkinson Asset Management approach to investing. We look for companies with a combination of four attributes: companies that are cheap versus their fundamental valuation; companies with earnings momentum; companies that have a strategy that has delivered high historic cash flow returns on investment; and stock momentum. We find that individually these attributes do not necessarily identify good stocks to invest in, but in combination provide a useful indication of those to look at.

My background has been well suited to investing in this area. First, I studied engineering at Cambridge University, which teaches all branches of engineering rather than focusing specifically on electrical or mechanical engineering. Understanding the technologies, and more important, the manufacturing processes used to build the products is essential to understand companies' ability to reduce costs and their exposure to specific input costs. I was also in the Energy & Utilities team in HSBC Investment Bank, which gave me a good understanding of the energy sector and how to value companies in the space. Third, as a merger arbitrage analyst in New York, I gained expertise in investment management. The focus on mergers meant that risk factors were an important part of the investment process, and I think this perspective is useful in an emerging sector like alternative energy.

The most interesting aspect of environmentally responsible work is that analyzing the sector gives you the information that cuts through the emotional hyperbole often employed in the environmental space. I also find it exciting that we are able to invest in stocks that will benefit as the entire world energy system is changed. I am optimistic that in my lifetime, we will see a dramatic shift in the energy infrastructure — we are seeing the beginning of that shift today. In the future, we all will be using much more energy than we do today, which will enhance global quality of living significantly. And the energy used will not be using up precious resources but harnessing the various forms of power from the sun, as solar, wind, hydro, wave, tidal, and biomass are all energy sources ultimately derived from the sun.

The biggest challenges I face in my work are the lack of real-time data and the reliance of the alternative energy industry on government support.

Much of the latest data we have to glean from discussions with market participants and doing primary research ourselves; it would be helpful if there were accurate sources of data on the sector, particularly in relation to pricing.

It is hard to criticize government support when it has been so important in getting the industry to the scale it is at today. However, the election cycle means different people are driving policy every few years, so you see dramatic shifts in subsidies and support levels over timeframes that are too short for changing our energy infrastructure. Excitingly, we are seeing the industry move to a point where a number of the technologies are moving beyond the need for government financial support — they mainly need structural support, such as a commitment to build appropriate infrastructure and guaranteed use of any energy produced. We expect this will move the case for alternative energy onto an economic footing (without subsidies), which is a much stronger platform for growth.

The global recession has not changed my work. I still spend a lot of time analyzing companies and the sector, but I think that investors' appetite to pay for future growth is low at the moment. This means that there are very attractive investment opportunities today in the alternative energy space if you believe that the sector will continue to grow.

The outlook for alternative energy has not changed dramatically — if anything, the case is even stronger today. We still are seeing high fossil fuel prices; fossil fuel reserves are not being replaced at a sustainable rate; and energy security concerns are only increasing as witnessed by the continuing turmoil in the Middle East.

As an Englishman, I find it difficult to dwell on my personal qualities, but I think the most important attributes for investing in the space are being able to think for yourself and asking questions that allow you to understand completely the companies in which you are investing. I have to be able to filter a huge amount of information, most of which is more opinion than fact. It takes a lot of hard work to cover the sector completely, and it is important to enjoy spreadsheets and numbers. Luckily, rational analysis gives me particular pleasure.

Our biggest challenge in this work is communicating the long-term story to investors. The strategy, like most areas, has been hit by the global recession, but in my opinion, that just makes it an even more attractive time to invest and take advantage of where current valuations are. We try hard to communicate our long-term outlook, and so far, we think we have managed to achieve that.

If anyone is interested in doing the same as me, they should first note that this is a highly competitive sector, which means it is even harder to break into than other areas of fund management. To become a fund manager in the sector today, a good approach would be to gain relevant industry experience by working at one of the major alternative energy companies or work as an equity analyst to learn about the sector, but even then, it would be a challenge. There are not currently very many alternative energy fund management jobs.

I also think a background in the conventional utility sector would be valuable. This is a much less-loved area, but it is an important sector to understand when looking at alternative energy. Solar panel manufacturers, wind turbine manufacturers, and many of the developers are selling their products to utilities. And the small renewable utilities are trying to become the mainstream utilities of the future. There are good lessons to be learned from the history of the utility sector that can be applied to what will happen in alternative energy. Our investment approach has stemmed from Guinness Atkinson's expertise in conventional energy investing, and we think that understanding the fundamental economics of all forms of energy is essential for analyzing the growth of the alternative energy sector.

Investing in Water

Investing in water can include small state-of-the-art companies developing stand-alone equipment for Third World areas, as well as major manufacturers such as General Electric and 3M who cater to the utility scale projects. Outside investment in water projects and technology is slow, and the industry is crying out for more venture capital. It seems that there was a rush to invest in renewable energy when green investing became popular, but with many startups becoming overvalued, cleantech, whether water or energy-related, became an investment that is heavily researched but not so readily supported.

Another reason funds have been limited in the water-investing field is that there are many different answers but no clear solutions, and many of the technologies do not appear to have the potential for high profits. For instance, even with the advanced technology of reverse osmosis, the market for RO membranes, the heart of the functionality, does not even amount to $1 billion each year. Thus, clean water is a much poorer prospect than renewable energy.

A further problem with water investment is that it takes a long time to go from a viable model to commercial application. Public water utilities have to be convinced before adopting new technology, and there is little reward for them to take risks and be at the leading edge. There is seldom any competition, as water utilities tend to have a monopoly in any particular area, and they adopt the attitude of "if it is not broken, it does not need fixing." This is coupled with the fact that many public water utilities have a fixed budget and are not keen to spend outside of their routine costs, and introducing clean water breakthroughs to the industry is a difficult task, which makes any returns for investors susceptible to delays and hard to come by. The truth is that water is a $500 billion industry that trails only electricity and oil in market size, but venture capital is limited to about $120 million per year.

With those provisos about the speed of adoption of any technology by industry, there is no doubt that water will become increasingly important, even though it may take a few crises before there is general acceptance of this. One thing is certain: the need for water can only increase, and it is not a discretionary purchase. Elster Solutions (**www.elstersolutions.com**), an English company, is a leading supplier of electronic water meters to the Gulf region and has recently released a smart water meter that has no moving parts, which means the meters are not susceptible to blockage. The company has supplied water meters to the area for the last 50 years and is proud that the meters are designed for harsh and hot operating conditions. Elster also produces gas and electricity meters.

One company that is hoping for the industry to concentrate on smaller, decentralized units, particularly in developing countries where infrastructure would be capital intensive and prohibitive, is Spectra Watermakers (**www.spectrawatermakers.com**) from California. The company was formed in 1997 and concentrated on marine uses such as drinking water purification for cruise and power boats for which it is still well known. However, it now makes land-based water treatment systems and sells a "Solar Cube" that provides an off-the-grid solution to supply water and electricity. This features solar-powered reverse osmosis, and the newest energy-efficient high-pressure pump requires less of the generated solar and wind power to operate. Spectra is a leader in using solar and wind power together with its RO and energy recovery products, and the systems are used for disaster recovery when the utility supplies have been disrupted, such as the 2005 Pakistan earthquake, as well as in remote areas.

One key that may mean Spectra Watermaker's success is that decentralization of water supplies represents a viable system to be adopted in many areas. As their units are small and self-contained, there is no need for any central organization, and this means that any problems or even terrorism will have less of an impact and involve fewer users. The company is refining its designs continually for more efficiency and energy recovery, which means each will produce more water and/or more power that can be put to other ancillary uses. Although Spectra is currently privately held, it is worth watching both as a potential sector leader and as a possible takeover target when a major company decides to get in on the business.

Aqua Sciences, Inc. (**www.aquasciences.com**) of Florida has developed an interesting approach to supplying clean water. Their equipment was deployed after the Haiti earthquake and became the primary source of water for the University Hospital in Port-au-Prince. They claim to produce 1,200 gallons of water per day from the humidity in the atmosphere. The company also supplies package units that include RO systems so any water on site can be purified. The unit can be self-contained with a diesel generator or served from a grid supply.

The other investing opportunities are in the infrastructure business. Much of the developed world has an old and deteriorating water distribution piping network, and the developing world needs to install a great deal of infrastructure. It will take severe shortages of water to occur more frequently before the developed world will wake up to the needs. Typically, entrepreneurs and emerging companies are looking toward the untapped markets of the developing world, and it is difficult to know which will succeed and prove worthy of investment. The other approach to investing in clean water is to review the large multinational companies' work to see how these can be invested in. Multinationals such as ITT, Siemens, and GE are involved with filtration and purification, typically by their previous purchases of smaller companies specializing in this area. There is a lot of activity in the clean water field, but some of it will not prove worth investment.

COMPANIES MENTIONED IN THIS CHAPTER

Hyflux (**www.hyflux.com**)

Elster Solutions (**www.elstersolutions.com**)

Spectra Watermakers (**www.spectrawatermakers.com**)

Aqua Sciences, Inc. (**www.aquasciences.com**)

Chapter 9

Green Building

To understand the different aspects of green buildings, it is necessary to start with what the purpose of a building is. Most would agree they protect us from harsh weather and that they provide a comfortable, safe, and, when necessary, productive environment. This includes the quality of the air, the temperature, the amount of light, and the provision of services such as drinking water and electricity. The green building will achieve these optimal conditions while aiming to have little or no impact on the environment.

A sustainable and green building can mean many things, though in whatever circumstances, it means adopting best practices. There is no one formula for generating a perfect sustainable building, and depending on the measures that are adopted, a sustainable property does not have to cost more than the conventionally made building. With increasing acceptance of this as a path to the future, it seems that green building may have a number of financial advantages.

According to a McGraw-Hill report from November 2010, the U.S. green building market is expected to reach $135 billion by 2015, about 8 percent of all construction. Other reports, such as that from *EL Insights* put the number higher, at $173 billion. Leadership in Energy and Environmental Design (LEED) has now become a recognized standard for evaluating the "greenness" of any building project, both in construction and in usage. The LEED certification program, developed by the U.S. Green Building Council (**www.usgbc.org**) and now in its third revision (v.3) provides third-party verification that a building is designed in a way that is cognizant of energy concerns, and professional designers, architects, and engineers can achieve qualifications to show they have studied how to become effective stewards of our environment. The LEED program was first developed back in 1998, and though it provides an excellent framework from which green

projects can be developed, it has gone through major revisions to make it more effective and increase its adoption. It is a voluntary standard, and as such, it had to fight for recognition so it would be viewed as something worth attaining and possibly paying a premium for. Consequently, the education of building owners and managers was a necessary part of pushing the agenda.

Green building seems to be positively impacting the amount of retention and turnover on leased buildings. Once landlords become confident of this, there will be more insistence on buildings being delivered that achieve LEED ratings, with the better ratings commanding higher rents. This also should mean property values are maintained over the long term, another incentive for green building. For the real estate investor, LEED certification is becoming a desirable attribute that can mean increased revenues.

When the U.S. has seemed to be so unaccepting of other green issues, with many in the population still in denial that it is man's actions that have led to climate change, it is somewhat surprising and forward thinking that this program has been available and in place for so many years. Perhaps it sprang from the United Nations resolve in 1987 that the world should achieve sustainable development, which was defined as "development that meets the needs of the present without compromising the ability of future generations to meet their own needs."

Several standards associated with the LEED program denote different levels of achievement. They range from being LEED registered to various levels of LEED certification, depending on the practices employed. The grades are called Certified, Silver, Gold, and Platinum, and each level requires more points or credits from a shopping list of property improvements. Canada recently has adopted a similar program that is modified to accommodate the particular needs of their environment and climate.

A sustainable and green building can mean many things, though in whatever circumstances, it means adopting the best building and construction practices. There is no one formula for generating a perfect sustainable building, and depending on the measures adopted, a sustainable property does not have to cost more than the conventionally made building. With increasing acceptance of this as a path to the future, it seems that green building may have a number of financial advantages.

Different Aspects of Green Building

The LEED program covers eight major areas of concern when evaluating sustainability. As such, it goes far beyond what many people would associate with this goal. The definitions and considerations have been developed over several years, and the current list includes some that may not be immediately obvious when considering sustainability. The concerns are summarized as:

- Location — the impact on the environment depends on where the building is located in relation to infrastructure.

- Sustainability of the site — whether it is previously developed or green field, the impact on erosion, storm water runoff, light pollution, etc.

- Regional priority — addressing the environmental concerns of the region in which the building is proposed

- Water efficiency — smarter use of water both inside and outside the building with considered landscaping

- Indoor environmental quality — not only the air quality but also natural light and acoustics

- Energy and atmosphere — both during construction and use

- Materials and resources — covering the sustainability of the materials used, reduction of waste and recycling

- Innovation in design — a catch-all topic for improving a building's environmental performance in ways that may not have been specified by LEED

The rating system specifically includes consideration of the location and planning of the building and features categories for the sustainability of the site and the regional priority. It is clear from the standards that there are good and bad places buildings can be established and that the overall consideration of this fact is important. From an investor's viewpoint, whether this is material depends on the type of portfolio being established, as some technologies will prosper regardless of the physical location, but a real estate portfolio would have location and suitability of the site as a major component.

Apart from these three criteria that are specific to the building location, there are factors that can be adjusted by design and choice. The most obvious of these include the efficient use of water and the establishment of satisfactory indoor air quality. These topics are open to developments in technology and bear closer scrutiny in establishing a green investing plan. The remaining topics of the eight reviewed include energy and atmosphere, materials and resources, and innovation and design process. Although more general in form than the previous two, these again represent opportunities to stay in touch with the latest research and advances in order to find profitable opportunities. The eight topics in total contribute to the LEED rating of the building, and attaining a good LEED rating is becoming a worthwhile goal as its popularity spreads.

It is a matter of fact that buildings considered energy efficient under LEED program ratings are easier for commercial landlords to rent and have a higher occupation percentage. A CoStar* study in 2008 found that LEED certified buildings had a 4.1-percent higher rental occupancy. They also are inclined to rent for more than non-LEED certified buildings. The same study found a rent premium of $11.33 per square foot over non-LEED buildings. Studies have shown that a LEED-certified building may cost 2 percent more than a simple Code-compliant one, but the savings are expected to be ten times that over the life of the building. They provide healthier environments that contribute to worker productivity and retention.

In addition to having many different grades of green building performance, the investor also is faced with many different groups of investment when it comes to green or sustainable buildings. Just as the definition of green building is awkward to pin down, so there are diverse aspects that reasonably can be associated with the term.

Energy efficiency

Perhaps the most obvious aspect of sustainable buildings, energy efficiency is the main selling point of a green building to owners and users. Practically every item that consumes energy in a building can be made more efficient, but it takes consistent effort to identify and isolate the worthwhile opportunities.

Considering where energy is used in the building, cooling the space is a major consumer, as might be expected. Air conditioning uses a lot of power, and improvements in this field in terms of efficiency are being made all the time. Tackling the problem from a different angle, another approach is to minimize the air-conditioning loads a building experiences so less powerful equipment is required. Any energy consumed in the building contributes to the heat load, so installing more energy-efficient equipment such as lighting means there is an energy savings not just in a reduced lighting electrical load, but also in a reduction in air-conditioning load. Certainly in winter there is a gain from light heat output that reduces the heating required, but this is not an example of getting something for nothing, as the heat has to be paid for whether it comes incidentally from lighting or purposefully from heating equipment.

Roughly, 50 percent of the power used in a building goes into mechanical work, such as driving the motors used in air-conditioning equipment. Lighting accounts directly for about one-fifth to one-fourth of the energy used. Incidental heating and heating water uses roughly one-sixth of the building energy consumed. The remainder is spent on incidentals such as electronics and cooking.

Energy efficiency is also the key in developing countries, such as China, where there is an enormous potential for achieving much better efficiencies in industrial motors, fans, chillers, and pumps, which tend to be used for a greater period of time and are replaced less frequently than those in the U.S. It is impossible and immoral to tell the newly created middle class in developing countries they should not have access to comfort conditioning in their homes or personal transportation as those in the U.S. have enjoyed for decades. The immediate need is for these developing countries, in particular, to progress as efficiently and cleanly as possible, particularly in the building field where the consequences of decisions made today will be lived with for many years, rather than following in the footsteps of the Western world with energy usage evolution.

There is a growing realization that saving energy is the equivalent of providing a new energy resource and must be treated as seriously as the issue of discovering more ways of producing clean energy. Often increasing efficiency in buildings is relatively unnoticed, as it is far less glamorous than installing solar arrays or a wind turbine, but it is equally worthy of our attention in the pursuit of clean energy.

Lighting

The topic of more efficient lighting was first discussed in Chapter 6. In that chapter, light bulbs were considered in isolation, and more efficient forms were discussed. But when considered in the context of green building, there are other options than replacing light bulbs. Perhaps the biggest and most obvious part of incorporating energy-efficient lighting is daylight, and several things can be considered when planning a green building.

There is a balance to be struck. If the building introduces too much daylight or introduces it in an inefficient way, it can be counterproductive. For instance, heat as well as light passes through windows, so designing a building with additional windows for increased daylight might result in a higher air-conditioning load despite reducing the need for artificial light. There are many aspects to this, as insulated windows with various heat-rejecting coatings can control the passage of heat without unreasonably restricting light. Some of these issues can be dealt with by careful building orientation.

There have been developments in the window technology that provide for more careful control of light and heat ingress. In the 1970s in England, British Gas pioneered research into automatic Venetian blinds that could sense the sun's angle and intensity and adjusted themselves throughout the day. This was sometimes to the amusement of the staff because the blinds would react noisily and frequently to the demands of their experimental control system.

Window construction

Forty years later, much better solutions are available. It is common knowledge that glass is a poor insulator, and that is why an ordinary window will feel hot in summer when the adjacent wall is still cool. This applies to some extent even with regular insulated glass, which has two panes with an air gap between them. The average home in the U.S. loses about one-third of its air-conditioning energy through windows.

The better and more expensive solutions are triple glazed windows that have reflecting surfaces, where the air gaps are filled with a gas such as argon that is a much better insulator than air. Without doubt, they pay for themselves when constructing new buildings and even can be worth using as replacements for existing windows where the additional costs can be recovered within about ten years. In new construction, the air-conditioning equipment may be smaller and give further gains.

Smart Windows

Naturally, technology has now come up with what are called "smart windows" that go one step further than conventional treated windows and provide either manual or automatic control of their shading abilities. There are several variations on this idea, with different manufacturers developing alternative ways to accomplish this. Electrochromism is possibly the most common of the technologies used to darken windows to restrict the entry of heat, but the common thread in all smart windows at the moment is that they are too expensive for widespread application.

Electrochromic windows control the amount of daylight and solar heat gain by darkening when a voltage is applied to them, which means they require an available power source. They stay dark when the voltage is turned off and can be lightened by reversing the voltage. For instance, by using a photovoltaic cell that reacts to light, in conjunction with each different facade of the building, voltage can be applied when sunlight is present. If the voltage is varied, the darkness of the window can be modulated. As the window stays dark even without a continuing voltage, this technology is efficient. In technical terms, a voltage is used to transport charged ions into an electrochromic layer, which changes its transparency. The active layers are sandwiched between two plates of glass. The reverse voltage acts to force the ions back into a storage layer, which lightens the glass. One drawback to the process is that it is slow; it takes a matter of minutes to change the darkness of a window. Another drawback is that the windows currently cost about $100 per square foot.

A company called Soladigm (**www.soladigm.com**), headquartered in Milpitas, California, recently announced a new process to make electrochromic windows and received $30 million of venture funding at the end of 2010. Soladigm calls its product Dynamic Glass, and some projections say it could cost as little as $20 per square foot. It is worth watching for advances and potential breakthroughs in this type of window control.

Another angle on window tinting comes from a company called RavenBrick (**www.ravenbrick.com**), which manufactures a film that can be applied to existing windows. The film requires no control system or electric current and has only two states: clear or darkened. The film darkens in response to heat, so in the winter it is totally clear. The Denver-based company calls the technology thermoreflective filters, and at the time of writing, it is undergoing government analysis. The General Services Administration (GSA), the landlord for many government buildings, has the technology under test at its Denver Federal Center.

Solar Tubes

Adding conventional windows is not the only solution to increasing daylight. Another idea that has value in specific applications is that of the light pipe. This goes under several different names, such as solar tube, and they all have the same operating principle as an opening on the roof that allows light to travel through a tube to the ceiling. There are various enhancements from different manufacturers. Some use mirrors or a mirror-finish pipe for better light transmission, and some even use optical fiber for flexibility. There is even a version that uses a light sensor to track the movement of the sun and maximize the light captured.

The only problem with using this feature is it depends on access from the roof to the ceiling and, thus, is largely unsuitable for multistory buildings. However, in buildings where they can be used, they are an excellent complement to windows and a replacement for electric light. Using lenses focuses and increases the benefit of the natural light, and there is less heat loss through the long tube than there is from conventional windows. Light can be "injected" into a room or interior space that is not near the perimeter of the building and offers no other way of providing natural light. The systems also can be combined with light sensors to maintain a relatively constant light level; thus, the electric lights only would be turned on when needed. The Alberta Research Council in Canada ran tests on typical light tubes and found the light output was equivalent to 1200 W of incandescent light. Most companies make two sizes, one to fit between joists spaced at 16-inch centers and a larger one that fits between joists spaced at 2-foot centers. The idea has been around in commercial form for about two decades and is still a minority notion, but the increasing emphasis on energy efficiency may result in growing acceptance.

Building materials

Another aspect of the LEED program is how buildings are constructed. The emphasis is on using easily renewable materials such as straw and bamboo, along with recycled materials, and achieving at least as good insulation as existing methods. There do not seem to be any leading manufacturers in these fields, as these solutions are offered on an ad hoc basis and not en masse. The building industry also has discovered lightweight sandwich polystyrene wall and roof panels that provide excellent insulation and ease of construction and are a replacement for conventional construction such as brickwork. Again, while it can be supplied in bulk mainly from Chinese manufacturers, it does not seem to have captured the public's imagination or the building marketplace at this time.

There is no one trait that categorizes any construction material as required for green construction, as it depends on the emphasis that is being placed on the various aspects. For instance, you may think insulation that is manufactured in an environmentally friendly manner is automatically a necessary component of green construction, but not all green buildings have super insulation. Each building must be examined on its merits. An old idea that is seeing some revival is that of thermal mass — constructing a building with heavyweight materials that will store heat during the day and release it at night when the temperature cools, which saves on energy costs. This is how an adobe building would even out the temperature changes in a desert.

However, it is necessary that any material used is sustainable and produced in an environmentally friendly way, as to do otherwise would run counter to the concept. Metal is considered a reasonably green building material on the basis that it can be recycled relatively easily when no longer required, is long lasting, and may even have reflective properties to help with environmental control in hot climates. For different reasons, bamboo is a popular green material, as it grows quickly and can replace other materials, such as wood from forests that are being depleted.

The Environmental Protection Agency (EPA) also recommends using recycled goods from other processes, such as foundry sand, debris from previous demolition, and other materials that can be sourced locally. However, because of the diversity of approaches to the subject of green building construction, there are not many opportunities for green investing in this field.

Residential Design

Although the LEED program is most commonly associated with commercial construction, residential users can reduce their energy consumption a number of ways, and this can even be a selling point for developers. For years, homeowners have taken action to reduce their fuel bills by installing insulated windows, by using front-loading washing machines, and by other common sense provisions. Nowadays, saving energy has taken on a new dimension, with super-efficient homes being built in new subdivisions.

One of these subdivisions is Vista Montaña in California. Built by Clarum Homes, it comprises nearly 400 living units ranging from apartments to single-family homes. The walls are built with a Styrofoam™ layer that greatly improves the insulation and with roof sheathing that blocks some of the summer heat. Many homes have solar PV panels that can supply most of the electricity requirements. A feature of this housing development is the use of tankless water heating, a system that long has been available in Europe. This heating system involves heating water only as it is needed, with no or minimal hot water storage, which avoids the heat loss associated with a conventional system. Producing instantaneous hot water requires a large heat input for a short time, and this usually is provided with a wall-mounted gas-fired heater.

Decades ago, these were looked upon as the cheaper form of water heating, and there were several deaths from asphyxiation as the heaters had open flames. They were called geysers or "Ascots" after the name of one of the manufacturers, and they were typically wall-hung in a bathroom. Although open flame appliances need a supply of outside combustion air, the tendency in a bathroom is to block off vents that may give rise to chilly drafts, and this was one reason for the malfunctioning that led to the fatalities.

The modern versions of these water heaters, now called tankless water heaters in the U.S., are much improved. A typical efficient unit is the Vertex™, manufactured by A. O. Smith. However, it is not likely that there will be a wholesale change to water heaters at the point of use as represented by this model, as there are several drawbacks.

- The tankless water heater needs a large electricity or gas supply in order to provide enough heat to the water as it flows. This may require upgrading a utility installation and certainly will need beefed-up supplies to the heater location.

- The heaters are typically at least twice the cost of conventional storage water heaters, and this cost differential can require many years, perhaps more than the 20-year lifetime of the unit, to recoup.

- Tankless water heaters are more prone to problems with scaling, and many experts advise a yearly clean and service, which commonly can be skipped with storage water heaters.

- The water can run hot and cold. Certainly when the heater starts, when the water is turned on, the first slug of water will be cold. Until water is flowing, the heater controls are unable to assess the heat that must be added to achieve an acceptable temperature.

- Further temperature difficulties are caused by water flow. If there is a low flow, perhaps for shaving, the heater may not ignite the gas. If the flow suddenly increases, perhaps with a washing machine or dishwasher drawing hot water while you are showering, you can expect an impact on the water temperature. Many units cannot cope with simultaneous demands, purely because of the rating.

- Although gas units usually are preferred, as it is easier to achieve the heat input needed, if you have an electric unit there will be no hot water available any time that there is a power cut — unlike a storage heater, which always can deliver the water that has been preheated.

These drawbacks do not mean tankless heaters do not have a future, particularly if there are grants and subsidies available to offset the high installation costs. However, they require consumers to think more about how they use hot water and perhaps to change their habits to suit the characteristics of the units. Tankless water heaters are more "high tech" than the conventional alternative and, thus, require an adjustment of attitude and expectation.

In the residential air-conditioning field, there may be big changes coming. For years, the basic residential air conditioner has been based on the same method of operation, called the vapor compression cycle. Over the years, it has been steadily made more efficient by engineers who have improved the design and refrigerants in response to more demanding government regulations. The cycle consists of the refrigerant being compressed by the compressor pump, which raises the temperature. This refrigerant is passed through a heat exchanger, normally outside the building and with a cooling fan passing air over it, which cools and condenses the refrigerant to a liquid.

The liquid is passed through a controlled expansion valve into another heat exchanger, this time inside. When the liquid expands, it becomes a gas and cools, giving the cooling needed for the air-conditioning function. The cycle then repeats, with the refrigerant being compressed and heating up again.

The only reasonable (and economical) alternative to this has been evaporative coolers that use the evaporation of water by air passing through wet pads to cool the temperature. Contrary to popular belief, these take no heat out of the air, although they do reduce the temperature. This is explained by the fact that they add moisture to the air by evaporation, and moist air with the same amount of "heat" is actually at a lower temperature. These units are not effective in all areas; they perform best in the dry atmospheres such as Arizona and Nevada deserts and do not work at all in moist climates such as Florida.

There is another widely used process for refrigeration, called absorption refrigeration, which actually reduces the heat in the air like the vapor compression cycle does. This has been used in larger commercial applications and where circumstances suited it. It works from a heat source, sometimes from rejected heat, such as that given off from power plants, and sometimes from a gas flame. This process is what allows refrigerators used in recreational vehicles to be powered by propane gas. It is generally more expensive and better suited to large air-conditioning applications.

The refrigerant is frequently ammonia on the large installations, and this "boils" or becomes gas at a low temperature when at atmospheric pressure but when used in the refrigeration cycle is kept at a higher pressure making it liquid at room temperature. In the same way as in the vapor compression cycle, the refrigerant is evaporated at room temperature, taking it from a liquid to gaseous state and cooling the indoor air. Instead of a compressor, the gas is then absorbed in another liquid, and heat in the mixture is rejected by cooling fins at the back of the gas-cooled refrigerator. Then the refrigerant is separated from the other liquid by heating by the heat source to allow the cycle to repeat. The whole process is generally not as efficient as the vapor compression cycle, but it is useful if you have heat that would otherwise go to waste. Because of the various functions included, the units usually cannot be made as compact as vapor compression units.

The reason you may want to know about the principles of the absorption refrigeration cycle is that nanotechnology is supposed to be transforming the situation shortly. The Pacific Northwest National Laboratory (**www. pnl.gov**) has reported that nanostructures, that is, substances that have a smaller than microscopic engineered structure, have been created. Because of this discovery, engineers are close to making an absorption unit that may halve the current costs, as well as being smaller. One exciting outcome for this is that the sun may provide the heat needed for the air conditioning, just when it is needed. Look for companies that are already in the nanotechnology field that may be looking at developing this idea, which could prove extremely lucrative when successfully implemented.

The Future for Green Buildings

The growth prospects for green buildings are enormous, as the idea finally has taken hold in recent years in the mainstream construction industry. In future years, we can look forward to most buildings being constructed and equipped using green and clean systems and materials. This is not only because of the savings in energy but also because paying attention to every aspect of building performance results in a better building product.

This fact has been recognized for several years. A review of LEED-qualified buildings conducted in 2003 found that they were not only on average 25 to 30 percent more energy efficient but also encouraged increased productivity from the occupants because of better temperature control, lighting control, and better indoor air quality. The extra cost for these benefits was estimated to be only a few percent more than conventional building.

However, unless you are a real estate investor, it may be difficult for you to partake of this growth. Very few stocks are significantly based on green building technologies and materials. Certainly, the control manufacturers for air-conditioning and lighting systems have a key role in green buildings, but this is currently only a small part of their business. The same applies to manufacturers of green building materials. The construction industry as a whole depends more on the state of the credit market and the world economy than on individual technologies, so the health of these producers is not closely related to how good their green products are. The companies mentioned in this chapter, together with others in the field, represent the choices available, but these are highly speculative, with little indication at this stage those that will be successful and that will fade away.

COMPANIES MENTIONED IN THIS CHAPTER

Soladigm (**www.soladigm.com**)
RavenBrick (**www.ravenbrick.com**)

Chapter 10

Transportation

he field of green or sustainable transportation is immense. The first thing that comes to many minds when the topic of energy-efficient transportation is discussed is a hybrid vehicle for personal transportation, but there are many other approaches to the issue of moving oneself and one's belongings around. Some require more adaptation than others, and all should be evaluated in trying to determine the future direction of the market. The goal of energy-efficient transportation is generally thought to be creating sustainable transportation, though definitions of this can vary.

A definition of sustainable transportation from the European Union Council of Ministers of Transport involves safe access to affordable transportation with competitive choices, with the key being limiting emissions and waste so the planet is able to absorb them. It also talks about using renewable resources within the rate of replacement and nonrenewable resources within the rate of development of other renewable substitutes. Although these intentions are laudable, and as a goal sound effective, in practical terms they give little indication which way the market will favor in the coming years, which is why a detailed set of alternatives are explained in this chapter.

In discussing the choices, it helps to have a "30,000-foot" view of the objectives. The cleanest and most sustainable form of transportation is available to most of us — simply walking. It is only when walking cannot fulfill the needs, such as when commuting several miles to work, that alternatives must be included. Even then, those alternatives can include self-powered options such as bicycles. Although nonpolluting in use, there may be a measure of ecological effect from the manufacturing process, but this would hardly register compared to the pollution of creating and using motorized forms of transportation. Despite the environmentally friendly nature of cycling, there are other problems, such as crowded cities and roads that pay

little attention to the cyclist and present safety hazards. With certain notable exceptions such as Portland, Oregon, where 6 to 8 percent of commuting is by cycle on 324 miles of bikeways, the cyclist must compete for space with far larger and heavier vehicles, and a revision to the infrastructure to reconcile this, even if pursued, would take some time.

The next logical step in the U.S. is to have an "efficient" automobile to transport yourself and others. This may mean purchasing cars with increased fuel economy or buying cars that use alternative fuel or energy to operate. Another option to consider when examining the notion of energy-efficient transportation is whether a personal vehicle is necessary. In Europe and some other countries, it is perfectly feasible to live without owning individual transportation and use mostly public transportation when necessary. In the U.S., this is impractical in most areas at this time. Public transport is another area to explore when looking for investing opportunities, even if it seems that the national habits would preclude much meaningful development of it.

Another approach to the environmental issues of transport is to eliminate the need for commuting, perhaps by telecommuting, but it appears that is a much-vaunted method that has failed to gain much traction in the years since its inception. However, there may be more pressure for its adoption as conventional transportation continues to get squeezed, and so there may be a technology growth area in the networking and virtual meeting field, which can be exploited by investing in hardware and software companies that take a lead in this direction.

The Least Disruptive Answers to Changing Transportation

It is in the nature of man to stick with the tried and true ways of doing things and to resist change. Despite the apparent urgency of reforming our lifestyles to reduce their deleterious impact on the planet and, hence, back to ourselves, many will be slow to take up the needed changes. When we look at something as deep-rooted in the societal psyche as our means of personal transportation, there are variations on how much we can continue in our ways relatively unaffected but with a reduced environmental impact. Although arguably an interim solution in the bigger environmental battle, by their nature, the least disruptive answers may be most readily and easily adopted.

Biofuels

Biofuels represent a modest change to current practices, as they are generally a substitute for existing fuels, and they are increasingly acceptable with little or no modification in modern vehicles. They have not always been judged a success in the U.S., particularly in 2009 when there was a glut of ethanol resulting from the increased production triggered by the previous year's high oil prices. This meant that those who had invested in ethanol production were faced with plummeting prices, and many companies found that it was uneconomic.

Many factors played into this disappointing foray of replacing oil with biofuel, in this case, ethanol. In retrospect, it is easy to see some basic problems waiting to happen. For one, the ethanol

Biodiesel

was to be made from corn, a perfectly good foodstuff, and if corn were to be diverted from the grocery store to ethanol manufacture then the simple economic equation of supply and demand would change the dynamics of the price calculation. The soaring price of oil, which made the ethanol production financially viable, had not become a long-term issue but was based on temporary market sentiment. The free market was also to blame in that many producers saw the opportunity for profit, which resulted in an oversupply of ethanol production plants. However, now the economy is back in order, so investing into this market has a bright, new future. The price of oil went down to $110 per barrel in 2014 from previous high prices, such as $145 in 2008. The number of ethanol-producing plants rose from 160 in 2008 to 211 in 2014. A depressed economy in the 2008 global recession added to its woes, but now there is much potential in investing in biofuels.

Investing in biodfuels once illustrated the problems of rapid expansion and shortsighted investment, but now this sector of the industry is undergoing consolidation in a more rational manner, but it would seem reasonable to suggest that corn-based ethanol might not be the most sensible way to go given the conflict with foodstuffs. The Environmental Protection Agency's decision in 2009 to increase the amount of ethanol required in gasoline also helped stabilize the market.

In 2007, the United States passed the Energy Independence and Security Act, which is designed to reduce the U.S. dependency on foreign imports. This act requires there to be 36 billion gallons of biofuels annually by 2022. This represents about 20 percent of the expected gasoline consumption. It requires more than half of the fuel to come from cellulosic processes and not use foodstuffs as a base. Cellulose is present in abundance in plants, in their cell walls, and is responsible for the strength of wood. Although it is made up of sugars, humans do not possess the enzymes to process it, so it is not considered a food so much as fiber or roughage in the diet. Cellulosic ethanol is exactly the same as ethanol produced from corn, but it comes from lignocellulose, which is based on a wide range of material such as waste wood chips, switchgrass, straw, and other sources — even agricultural waste can be used to make cellulosic ethanol. Because of this, it can be made from material grown across the country, rather than depending on areas favoring corn production.

Now before going any further, it is worth pointing out that although biofuels may be a sustainable energy solution in the right circumstances, some may argue that they are not necessarily the cleanest of options. Substituting one fuel for another still results in fuel being consumed, which causes at least some carbon dioxide release even if the actual fuel burns cleaner than traditional fuels, for example, by emitting less of the byproduct pollutants, such as sulfur dioxide. Proponents point out that the carbon dioxide produced is actually equivalent to the amount absorbed by the growing plants, effectively making the process carbon neutral, which means it, in effect, adds no carbon dioxide pollution to the air. This topic is complex in view of the time it may take to grow and consume different substances. If additional crops are raised purely for fuel, presumably the overall amount of carbon dioxide in the atmosphere will be depleted while the crops are growing. Regardless of the merits of this argument, there is no doubt that it is a solution that is immediately available for many current vehicles, which have been designed to burn flex fuel.

The flex fuel currently available, E85, is a blend of 85 percent ethanol and 15 percent gasoline, and flex fuel capable engines have been produced since the 1980s. It is likely that many owners and drivers do not even realize their vehicles are capable of using this fuel, as all flex fuel engines operate normally on what we now know as gasoline, which commonly comes with 10-percent ethanol anyway (this mixture used to be called gasohol). All gasoline engines produced since 1988 have been capable of burning gasoline with 10 percent ethanol. The first vehicle available that could use either gasoline or ethanol, or a mixture of the two, was the Ford® Model T.

The reason that the percent of ethanol is limited to 85 in the U.S. market is that the gasoline portion helps prevent problems with the engine starting at low temperatures. In the Brazilian market, which is leading in adoption of alternative fuel vehicles, cars are produced that can use 100 percent ethanol. This has been achieved by design development, though in the early days, this was achieved by separate injection of gasoline during starting.

Using E85 is not without its problems however. Ethanol has less energy, which means that fuel consumption goes up, and you get about 15 percent less in your miles per gallon calculations. Ethanol is a little cleaner than gasoline, but because you are using more ethanol per mile, the net pollution per mile remains similar. It currently costs slightly less per gallon, but with the reduction in mileage, it is more expensive to use E85 than regular pump gasoline. E85 is an established standard, so will not be replaced or superseded soon, but other forms of biofuel may be developed in the future that can gain a foothold in the marketplace.

Other than its general adoption at the present time, there is no reason E85 will remain a contender in the sustainability field. Another biofuel consumers can use that requires little change from existing habits is biodiesel. In the U.S., diesel-powered vehicles are not common for personal transportation, but in other countries, they have found favor, and this has resulted in modern diesels sounding and behaving differently from those Americans may have been used to. The popularity of diesels has spread particularly in Europe where fuels are expensive and where the better economy of the diesel cycle helps to balance the additional cost of purchasing a diesel car.

Although there are tales of individual entrepreneurs running their vehicles with waste oil, such as old restaurant frying oil, this solution cannot be widely adopted because of the limited availability of such products. For commercial production of biodiesel, the U.S. market tends toward soybean oil, and the Europeans use rapeseed (canola) oil. This, again, highlights the difficulty in determining where the market winners will come from, as investing in particular technologies can mean you miss out on the ultimate victor. Some companies are determined to win regardless of the future direction, as they are large enough to be diversified in several directions. One such company is the Archer Daniels Midland (ADM), more commonly known through its advertising as the supermarket to the world. It is a leader in agricultural goods, processing and marketing them, which puts it in a good position to choose the types of crops that can be processed into biofuel. ADM (**www.adm.com**) is taking advantage of its size, position, and knowledge to become heavily involved in the upcoming biofuel industry. It has many other products, so is not a pure green energy play by any means. However, it is a big player in the biofuel market with ethanol production in the U.S. in the region of 13 billion gallons a year. The diversity in other fields also can help protect it from energy price fluctuations. Having made massive investments in recent years in new plants for biofuel production, ADM is exposed to the risk of oversupplying the market and consequential falling prices, but the sheer size of the company and its diversity will mean it can ride out any such periods.

Another company that may have a future in the biofuel industry is Imperium Renewables (**www.imperiumrenewables.com**). At the time of writing, this company is still in private hands and is funded by venture capitalists, hedge funds, and private equity. In the past, there were plans for an initial public offering (IPO) to take the company public, but these were shelved. The funds would have gone toward three production plants to expand on their existing two plants, the larger one of which has a capacity of more than 100 million gallons per year. It has the largest certified production facility in the U.S. and makes biodiesel from vegetable oil grown in the Northwest; it had to cut back on its earlier plans to use palm oil from Southeast Asia in the face of criticism that this would cause further destruction of the rainforest. Although worth watching, Imperium Renewables may end up missing the opportunity to compete with the major producers such as ADM. The business has been volatile, with the cancellation of a contract with Royal Caribbean in 2008 that caused layoffs, some of whom subsequently have been rehired. If Imperium Renewables does come to the market, it will be necessary to evaluate fully the potential for biodiesel at that time before deciding whether to invest.

Biofuels are now picking up progress and could potentially be the way of the future. A few years ago, jatropha, which is a hardy drought-resistant perennial plant, was a much-touted route, and BP was involved in a joint venture to plant 3 million acres of it in Africa. But just a couple of years after this, BP abandoned it to concentrate on ethanol, which is made from sugar cane in Brazil; switchgrass in the U.S.; and on another fuel, bio-butanol. It was reported that the crop from jatropha was unreliable, so even though it can be grown on marginal land unsuitable for general agriculture, it was not thought to be viable in comparison with alternatives. Add to this the fact that it is toxic and hard to work, and the initial enthusiasm for it has departed. Some still believe it can be useful for preventing soil erosion and restoring nutrients to poor soil, but it does not appear to be the savior first thought. As for bio-butanol itself, it is being plugged as a second-generation biofuel, as it has a higher energy density than ethanol and may become the next popular biofuel for gasoline-based engines. Although it has a higher energy density and, thus, restores some of the fuel economy of a vehicle, and it can be used almost directly in gasoline engines without such extensive modifications as are required for ethanol, there are some disadvantages to be overcome. First, it is still expensive to produce and so is not commercially viable yet. Production requires fermentation of biomass such as sugars and starches, and there may be issues with starting a cold vehicle. Research is trying to address all these issues, and, at this time, it remains to be seen whether bio-butanol can become a serious competitor. Curiously, the nonbiological version, butanol, until recently had been produced from petroleum.

Hybrid vehicles

The Toyota Prius was the first mass-produced hybrid car, so-called because it combined electric drive and internal combustion power in one system. With a system that charges the batteries when the driver uses the brakes, the fuel economy is actually better in the city than on the open road, a reversal of normal expectations, though it is equally at home in either environment. Since 1997 when it was introduced in Japan, the world has changed with increasing gas prices. The hybrid car is much less of a novelty and more of a genuine alternative to conventional vehicles. The chief problem is that it is not a real solution to the world in which we find ourselves, because it still causes direct pollution. It may be thought of as an interim solution on the path to other technologies.

Despite this, it is expected that hybrid technology, rather than pure electric power, will be the first choice of many for years to come. For instance, Ford believes that by 2020, as much as a quarter of its sales will have some form of electric drive but that 75 percent of those sales will be hybrid rather than pure electric. In 2011, there is an impressive array of hybrids, from Hyundai*, Ford, Infiniti*, Lexus*, Volkswagen, Kia*, and others. The range of vehicle types is increasing, with something for every taste.

The Toyota Prius represents just one step, as a hybrid electric vehicle. At present, it has no capacity to be plugged in to the electric network, and the small gasoline engine is used to charge the batteries and supplement the power, giving better gas mileage. It seldom operates purely from the batteries without the engine providing some work. The newly introduced Chevy Volt, on the other hand, takes the idea of a hybrid vehicle to another stage, as it is a plug-in hybrid vehicle. This means that you can charge it at home or at a charging station as they become available. The snag is that it can only travel 40 miles in an all-electric mode before recharging. After that, the gasoline engine has to come on. However, this might be suitable for some commuters who would only need the engine for longer weekend trips.

With government incentives, the economics of these vehicles are not too bad, but when you consider that a hybrid vehicle requires two distinct means of transmitting the power to the road for the two chosen power plants, it is no surprise that the vehicles are expensive. Add to this the more complex control technology required to manage the system reliably and select the economic mode of operation, and you have already added layers of complication to a motorcar, which translates into additional cost. The hidden killer for many owners is the cost of replacing a battery pack, which can be several thousand dollars and that has no real equivalent in a conventional car.

Electric vehicles

Going one stage further, it is now possible to buy commercial cars that run solely on electricity. This is seen as another step forward, although there is currently no national system in place that would allow you to take a long journey with minimum interruption in one of these. The problem is that there is no general standard or even easy access for the battery pack, which means you cannot reasonably exchange a depleted one for a freshly charged version at your local filling station and that recharging will take a certain time, even though some fast charging devices now are being developed.

These points hint at possible future developments to make the limitations acceptable. There have been proposals to invent a standard battery pack that could, for instance, easily be lowered from the vehicle, and a fully charged one substituted as a replacement, perhaps with little more difficulty than filling a gas tank. This idea has many debatable aspects — apart from the size of the initial process of making and equipping service stations with all these batteries, there are differing sizes depending on the size of vehicle and its designed range on a full charge. A small about-town runabout might want a compact and light battery pack that would be unable to power a larger utility vehicle more than a few miles. We are a long way from agreeing a standard or implementing such a scheme.

Fast charging is the alternative that would allow the user to travel distances greater than the range of the battery pack. There are technical issues to this, as the rate at which a battery can be charged must be limited to a safe level. The charging process can generate heat and damage the battery. Any fast-charging process would require special high-capacity receptacles, as the household type of receptacle is not capable of passing the required amount of energy safely. There are many variables to be balanced and evolved before there is any established standard for this potential solution. However, standard charging stations are being developed and will be spread across the country shortly.

But considering that most car journeys are short distances, the all-electric vehicle can be a transportation solution that requires little adaptation of current driving habits. The cars currently in the mass market in mid-2011 include the Nissan Leaf™, but many other smaller manufacturers and start-ups are not bound by conventional automotive factories and thinking, and they are exploring innovative solutions. It seems that electric car manufacturers are springing up all the time, and inevitably, some will fail and others succeed.

Here are some of the competitors. The Tesla (**www.teslamotors.com**) is one of the most exciting ranges of all-electric vehicles and has been available for sale since 2008 after five years of development. There are 1,500 Teslas currently on the road, making this a "boutique" rather than a mass-market product. In a no-compromise design, the Roadster Sport version is a genuine sports car, with a 0-60 mph time of 3.7 seconds and a top speed of 125 mph. Even so, the range between charges is far better than most electric cars at 245 miles, due no doubt to its custom lithium cell battery which has 6,831 individual cells. All this performance means the car is priced from $109,000 upwards, but there is still a waiting list.

Tesla has plans to produce a range of vehicles and will shortly announce a sedan. The sedan is rumored to be much cheaper and represents Tesla's attempt to become a much more mainstream manufacturer. There has been insider buying, with the CEO Elon Musk spending more than $40 million of his own money buying shares at market price in June 2011. Against this, other insiders have been selling, giving a mixed message, which possibly reflects the degree of uncertainty on whether the company will be able to expand and thrive. Insider buying normally is considered more significant than selling, as buying can only be in anticipation of profit whereas selling can be just for personal reasons, such as to get cash to buy a house or car.

Most electric vehicles in production do not have the performance of a Tesla Roadster in terms of speed, acceleration, or operating range between charges. For example, the Nissan Leaf ($32,000) has a range of 100 miles and a top speed around 90 mph; the Mitsubishi i MiEV already on sale in Japan will be offered in the U.S. in late 2011 at nearly $30,000 and has a 100-mile range and an 80 mph top speed. Generally, all-electric vehicles are more expensive than gasoline-powered vehicles due to the cost of the batteries, and these need total replacement after a number of years. Tesla estimates a 7-year life and a replacement cost of $12,000. It is possible to get large tax offsets to help with the initial costs. The Federal Tax Credit is currently $7,500 for each vehicle, with a phasing out as more units are sold.

There are many other small manufacturers, and these are mainly focused on the European and Japanese markets for now. They tend to offer smaller vehicles that are more acceptable in those particular markets. In fact, some of the vehicles seem to offer little more in speed or room than re-engineered golf carts, and may be restricted in performance to the extent that they would not be permitted on U.S. highways.

There are other questions raised about all-electric vehicles. For instance, although the operation is without emission or pollution, the electricity used to charge them may be and probably is produced with polluting technologies. The actual cost to the consumer may be about one-third of using gasoline, though the price of electricity varies widely. Whether gasoline or electricity is a more expensive way of powering your car may be a moot point if the operation does nothing for clean power. The Department of Energy (DOE) commissioned a survey to try to assess this factor.

The study considered the mix of generating sources for each of 13 regions of the country, and the conclusion is that a battery-only vehicle operating in New York would cause an increase in net pollution because of the generating source of electricity, with overall carbon emission up by 19 percent. In Greater Illinois, using a battery-powered vehicle would cause 36 percent more pollution, at least as far as pollution caused by the vehicle was concerned. Even a hybrid would cause nearly 12 percent more carbon emissions in this area, in which 75 percent of the electricity is generated by coal, and this was the worst in the country. The calculations are complex, as they must take into account the time of day that the car is charged and how it is driven, and there may even be an impact on necessary generating capacity if electric cars are widely adopted. In areas of the country that use fewer fossil fuels for generating electricity, the figures will work out better, though the most eco-friendly option would be to use solar panels mounted on your garage. If you are considering investing in some aspect of hybrid or electric transportation, there is the chance that sales could be set back by public awareness of this coming to the fore. The counter argument would be that using an electric vehicle positions the consumer to have a cleaner profile in a time when changes are made to power generation, and it is a vital first step to greening transportation.

One of the changes that could help is being put forward by GE, which has developed a product called an Electric Vehicle Solar Carport. This has a solar panel roof that feeds directly into a GE Smart EV Charging Station. This would provide a true clean-tech alternative for keeping your car charged up at home or at work. There is no single way to invest in this separately from the main company, but it is good to know that a major business is trying to include green technology where it can.

The Disruptive Solutions

The disruptive solutions are those where we need to put ourselves out in order to continue pursuing previously established ways of living, but in a greener way. In time, society also may change as suggested in New Concepts below, allowing green factors to be attained more easily.

The Segway®

The Segway (**www.segway.com**) is an idea that has yet to capture the imagination of the majority of the country. It is a fascinating use of engineering to ease personal transport and parking issues, but it has not been able to make much headway in its present form.

For those who have not yet seen one of these devices, it is a two-wheeled motorized electric scooter that costs $5,000 or more and is self-balancing. The surprise is that the wheels are side by side, rather than one in the front and one in the back like a conventional scooter. The Segway has been available since 2001, with an upgraded model in 2006, and it still has difficulty being accepted as a viable mode of transport. It is not allowed on sidewalks (pavements) in the United Kingdom and some other countries, as it is classified as motorized transportation, but it is not allowed on the streets, as it does not meet safety standards. The only place it can be used legally is on private property. In the United

States, most states have legislation that allows its use on sidewalks and bicycle paths, but the user always must check for restrictions and limitations.

Although this is one extreme, there are many issues getting this form of transportation accepted in most countries, and even the question of where it belongs. With a top speed of 12 mph, it is too slow to be safe on the open road, but too fast to mix safely with pedestrian traffic. Where it is allowed in cities, it is reportedly an excellent vehicle for a short commute that avoids the traffic holdups, and it can even be driven around inside buildings, and into elevators. The range is only 24 miles, but in any case this amount of commuting standing up in the elements is more than most people would be happy with. It truly is a novel solution just looking for acceptance and incorporation into daily use, but generally it is relegated to guided city tours and tours of Disney theme parks, with little hope of widespread use in this implementation.

The bicycle

Worthy of a mention, but still a means of transportation that is not widely accepted as a viable alternative to the motor car, the bicycle is not an satisfactory answer for many people for various reasons. Although it may be a healthy alternative to motorized solutions, the rider needs to have a basic level of fitness for regular use, and this coupled with exposure to the elements and difficulty in hilly areas means that the bicycle is not likely to experience resurgence for green reasons. Any investment in bicycle companies would not be based on anticipation of clean-tech boom.

The New Concepts

Given the difficulty of sustaining our current ways coupled with pursuing a green future, some advocates are saying our habits need to change to accommodate the new paradigm of clean living. This would require us to alter the ways in which we live our lives and what transportation we use or have access to. Most of these would have considerable opposition, as people always will resist change, so it is not likely that any will come to pass soon. The ultimate goal would be that any transportation required for our lives, including personal transportation and deliveries, would take place in a fully sustainable manner.

Some solutions to the transportation issues would not even involve transportation. After all, reducing the carbon impact of vehicles can be achieved by not using those vehicles. Telecommuting has been referred to above, and another change could be for office workers to be located in local centers. The idea is that the social and physical needs of office workers — computers, internet, telephones, photocopiers and the like — can be assembled in local offices, and regardless of the company for which you work, you attend the nearest center. Any interaction with colleagues in the same business increasingly can become "virtual" given the technology of the Internet, as documents can be shared and meetings held as if the participants were in the same room. As you are not working at home, with all the distractions that offers, and you are in a professional environment, there are fewer reasons for employers to object to this virtual placement and worry that they may not be getting value for their money.

This method of local working has many advantages — for instance, it is conceivable that you would not need to move when changing jobs, and that would save additional transportation and pollution as well as keeping children at the same schools. But the infrastructure and change of mindset required would take a long time to develop.

Another option to reduce transportation needs is to buy produce that has been grown locally, reducing the moving of goods. Although not everyone lives within easy access of agricultural land, in the next chapter you will learn of an idea where food is grown hydroponically and within easy distance of the place that it is needed. Again, this may not happen on a large scale soon, but it is an indication of the type of thinking that needs to take place to help with a greener future for the world.

If transportation is needed despite the economies of movement referred to above, many new concepts are put forward every year, but none has yet gained traction. An alternative in cities, which has had modest acceptance, is some form of overhead monorail system, and this is usually less disruptive and less costly than the popular idea of a light rail system, which is being built in places such as Phoenix, Arizona.

Monorail and bullet train

One of the proposals for mass transit in Phoenix, before the light rail system was decided upon, consisted of individual monorail cars, each of which would travel overhead down the center of existing roads. What made this system different was that the cars would be computer controlled and integrated together and would only descend to one of the stations positioned every mile if it was the occupant's destination. The next empty car would pick up any waiting passenger.

This allowed the system to provide nearly taxicab convenience to users, picking up and putting them down within easy distance of their destination, without the delay and inconvenience of everyone being forced to stop at stations along the way. It is an advanced concept, yet to be fully proven and only possible to implement safely because of modern computers — but it would make "mass transit" personal and much more acceptable to many people. If any company manages to achieve general acceptance of the principle demonstrated in practice, then it would be an exciting and probably profitable investment.

In the meantime, Phoenix commuters, in common with many others in metro areas, have access to a light rail system that is cheap, with much less environmental impact than individual car driving, but that is too inconvenient to persuade many motorists to give up their cars. It helps but does not provide a comprehensive solution.

COMPANIES MENTIONED IN THIS CHAPTER

Archer Daniels Midland (**www.adm.com**)
Imperium Renewables (**www.imperiumrenewables.com**)
Tesla (**www.teslamotors.com**)
Segway (**www.segway.com**)

Chapter 11

Agriculture

griculture is involved in many aspects of green investing. In this chapter, the emphasis is on agriculture for foodstuffs; other growing, such as crops for biofuels, planting for carbon trading, and other aspects are dealt with elsewhere. As much as progress has been made to work the land more intensively over the years by adding more fertilizers and pest controls, often made from oil, it is plainly obvious to a world observer that the population has far outpaced the land's ability to supply. According to the United Nations, the world's population is 7 billion. In 2050, assuming average growth, it will be more than 9 billion, or nearly 10.5 billion according to the higher growth estimates. If fertility remains constant, the figure works out to an even higher 11 billion. That is an almost 50-percent increase in less than 40 years. The fact is that we cannot even maintain our current existence unless there are changes. Areas that can be called deserts are expanding, and land is degrading, particularly in the poorer areas of the world where they cannot afford to take measures to protect the land. Chapter 8 talked about the shortage of clean water for drinking and for agriculture and how water will become more expensive, which inevitably will increase the cost of crops.

Farming has become more specialized, and rather than a natural rotation of different crops, some of which are less profitable than others, the tendency is for planting just a few productive and profitable varieties of crops year after year and replacing the soil nutrients chemically. Apart from the erosion of topsoil that results from these habits, such practices also bring the threat of more intense and devastating diseases because the soil has no rest period and no change of crop.

It is a similar picture in the fishing industry, where there is a general decline in the number of fish naturally available, in some cases dramatically so. It seems to be the result of further efficiencies, this time with regard to factory fishing catching vast quantities of fish, and methods of fishing that catch or damage types and sizes of sea creatures that are not the target. The United Nations published a recent report, "The State of World Fisheries and Aquaculture," which highlighted the problems. The world meanwhile is developing an increasing demand for fish, which at one time seemed so plentiful it was unbelievable that it could run out. Karl Almås, the president of SINTEF Fisheries and Aquaculture, Europe's largest research institution, has been quoted as saying that there is a huge gap between the world demand for fish and what we can harvest from natural resources. He sees a need to double the production of farmed fish in the next twenty years.

So, without some sustainable and clean-tech revision, it seems that continuing to work in the same ways will result in a declining food output, increased starvation in the world, and an increasingly desperate situation. This chapter will review different approaches to agriculture and food supply to see where the future may lie.

Genetic Modification

Genetic modification (GM) is a highly contentious topic, as many people perceive it as messing around with food, a necessity of life. It is thought that because the whole science is so new, the long-term effects of launching genetically altered living material onto the earth are unknown. The effects may not be limited to the particular crops that are modified, but also spread to adjacent plants, and it may prove impossible to call back any alterations that may have a detrimental effect. The concern is so great that Europe has banned some GM foods almost entirely, but in other parts of the world,

GM has been widely adopted. For instance, in the U.S., 86 percent of the corn, 93 percent of the cotton, and 93 percent of soy grown is genetically modified. Another 9 million farmers in developing countries use genetically modified seed.

Although GM may not be universally embraced, there

is some precedent for altering the genetics of plants. This has been happening for centuries when farmers carefully select seeds that have desirable traits and hope that they will pass these traits on to the next crop. By doing so, farmers have been modifying their crops genetically, sometimes to the extent that the cultivated vegetable bears little resemblance to the original wild forebears. But arguably, GM as practiced in modern farming is wielding a far greater capacity for change. It was the discovery of deoxyribonucleic acid (DNA) in the last century that first showed scientists that they could affect plant's individual cells and do so relatively simply rather than using the blunt but natural instrument of cross-pollination. This has accelerated the progress of "designer plants" massively. These plants may be virtually identical to the previous generation with the exception of a single cell or trait.

As you might expect, one of the traits many are seeking in genetically modified plants is to make the plant more pest resistant. This saves the farmer from having to spray pesticide at the first sign of infestation, and thus, there is no fear of pesticide being carried into the food. Because the farmer does not have to spray, there is no need to make sure this is done several weeks before harvest, as is conventional practice. One such crop, for instance, is based around *Bacillus thuringiensis*, commonly called Bt. This bacterium was discovered at the start of the 20th century, is considered a biological alternative to a pesticide, and has been used as such since the 1920s. In 1995, the Environmental Protection Agency (EPA) approved the GM version of potatoes containing Bt, and this form of Bt is now used in several other crops such as cotton and corn. Far from being a scary prospect, Bt has been used as a separate spreadable product for nearly a century. In fact, Bt has been used in organic farming for many years as a microbial pest control. Having a crop modified to generate its own bacterium means there is no risk of overspray and that the delivery of the pesticide to the insects is direct and certain.

In a similar vein, plants have been modified to become herbicide resistant. The prevalent form of this is called Roundup˙ Ready˙, which refers to the popular herbicide Roundup. It used to be that farmers had to spray herbicides before crops sprouted because the herbicides could harm plant growth. After the crops are growing, they could be damaged or contaminated by any exposure to the herbicide. So, without chemical treatment, weeds had to be allowed to proliferate and compete with the crops, which reduced the yields. The advantage of the developed herbicide-resistant plants is that they can be sprayed with the particular product or herbicide for which they are designed at any time without endangering the crop.

Another use of genetic modification is to increase yields and to speed maturation. There is ongoing research regarding increasing nitrogen intake, which will lead to less need for artificial fertilizer. ArborGen˙ is a leading supplier of tree seedlings; they sell approximately a quarter billion seedlings every year. They are actively pursuing modifications to tree biology to allow faster growth and, hence, quicker replacement of the tree stock.

Many other features can be implemented using GM. Plants can be modified to cope with different climates, such as increasing drought tolerance for the poorer agricultural areas of the world and helping salt resistance as clean water becomes harder to find and more likely to be contaminated. The reason that GM has become so popular in the U.S. may come down to a simple Supreme Court decision in 1980 (Diamond v. Chakrabarty), when it was decided it was possible to patent biological life, provided it was "manmade." The patent actually involved the development of a type of bacteria that could ingest oil, but the principle has meant that GM crops can be protected legally, which means the research pays big dividends.

Monsanto is the recognized leader in the field, with a dominant position that has even seen the company purportedly threaten legal action against farmers whose adjacent fields show some evidence of the genetically engineered grain. However, the future of genetic modification is still under a cloud, even though its proponents assert it is the only way the world will be able to cope with feeding its population. In a sense, it is in the same position as a nuclear power, with advocates determined to prove its necessity and opponents fearful that there will be unforeseen consequences that cannot be controlled. For a view of the disadvantages of GM, a simple Internet search will reveal many websites such as **www.gm.org** from Genetically Modified Foods, an official blog that presents current news.

There is no doubt that there is a lot of money in genetic modification, which also is being undertaken on animals as well as crops. Practicality may dictate that farming continues along this path, though it depends on how much adverse publicity is forthcoming in the next few years. The majority

of GM work centers around a few large companies that can be expected to fight hard against any detrimental reports. For the investor, the main companies are Monsanto (**www.monsanto.com**), DuPont* (**www.dupont. com**), and Dow Chemical (**www.dow.com**) in the U.S. In Europe, Bayer* of Germany (**www. bayer.com**) is a major player, along with Syngenta* in Switzerland (**www.syngenta.com**). You must then make an individual assessment whether they can be expected to continue reaping the profits and whether genetic alteration is something with which you wish to be involved.

The alternative to investing in the GM leaders is to look at smaller companies that may flourish in the natural and organic food markets. Companies you could consider include the Hain Celestial Group (HAIN, **www. hain-celestial.com**), perhaps best known for its Celestial Seasonings° teas, and United Natural Foods (UNFI, **www.unfi.com**), a relatively large distributor. Hain Celestial sells conventional foods along with organic and "natural" foods, and this has allowed them to grow at a faster rate than conventional-only suppliers. UNFI is in the very competitive field of distribution and recently has said that it expects its margins to narrow. Both have outpaced the general market index but have hit the doldrums in 2011. The market for natural foods in general is increasing, but the higher prices tend to make consumers compromise when recession hits and times are hard.

CASE STUDY: CLEAN TECHNOLOGY IS READY FOR PRIME TIME

John Rubino
Green trader, analyst, and columnist

John Rubino is the author of Clean Money: Picking Winners in the Green-Tech Boom *(Wiley, 2008) and coauthor, with GoldMoney's James Turk, of* The Collapse of the Dollar and How to Profit From It *(Doubleday, 2007). His previous books include* How to Profit from the Coming Real Estate Bust *(Rodale, 2003) and* Main Street, Not Wall Street *(Morrow, 1998). After earning a finance MBA from New York University, he spent the 1980s on Wall Street, as a Eurodollar trader, equity analyst, and junk bond analyst. During the 1990s, he was a featured columnist with* TheStreet.com *and a frequent contributor to* Individual Investor, Online

Investor, *and* Consumers Digest, *among many other publications. He currently manages DollarCollapse.com and writes for* CFA Magazine.

Over the past decade, especially as a columnist with the financial website TheStreet.com, I covered the rise of clean technologies and the companies that were arising in the field. One of the things that became clear from this research was that a lot of the main clean technologies such as solar, wind, and smart grid were finally, after decades of gradual improvement, ready for prime time, and that they were emerging just as the world's governments were concluding that 1) they needed to spend a lot of money to keep their economies from falling into depression and 2) upgrading their energy infrastructure is a politically popular way to spend this extra money.

So, the conditions were in place for public money to drive the adoption of alternative energy sources, water management tech, and pollution control for the next few years. After that, their continued efficiency improvement would make them viable without the aid of government subsidies. So, they were looking at bull market with very long legs.

Among the clean technologies, the best prospects are:

Solar. The sun's energy is free, and as solar cells become more efficient at turning light into electricity, they will become more and more viable. Next generation thin-film solar cells are cheap and flexible and will cover a growing number of sunny climate rooftops going forward.

Smart grid. The addition of information technology to power grids will make the grids more flexible and cheaper. At a cost per unit of energy saved, that is far less than the cost of building new power plants.

Geothermal. Using the heat generated by the Earth's core to produce electricity is cheap, clean, and possible in many places around the world.

Next generation batteries. These will make electric cars and home-based power storage possible, which will revolutionize the global economy.

Aside from the investment angle, the most interesting part of cleantech is that it also offers one of the few employment markets with good growth prospects. So, it is reasonable to expect the field to attract many of tomorrow's best and brightest and to be the source of high-paying, high-profile work that has the added advantage of changing the world for the better. The scientists and engineers who develop the next generation of cleantech will be revolutionaries in the most positive sense of that word. They will have the rare chance to do very well by doing good.

The biggest problem faced by cleantech and the people associated with it is that most of these technologies still depend on government subsidies and tax incentives, which can disappear with the stroke of a pen. That makes them inherently vulnerable in a way that most other industries are not.

Another risk facing cleantech, perhaps more than any other industry, is disruptive innovation. There are breakthroughs pouring out of labs around the world, many of which could, if they live up to their early hype, make whole sections of the alternative energy and other clean fields obsolete. To take just a few examples, several new battery designs appear to offer dramatic advantages over currently available models, while new thin-film solar modules are generating results that surpass anything now on the market. This is a huge risk for anyone hitching their star, financial or career, to an existing player in this field.

Today's economic problems are far more serious than just another recession. To put it concisely, the U.S., Europe, and Japan have spent the past three decades borrowing ever greater amounts of money to fund military empires (U.S.) and massive social welfare systems (everyone). Now, we are functionally broke, with only two remaining choices: to collapse under the weight of all this debt or try to inflate it away by destroying the value of our currencies. This will end very, very badly.

For cleantech in this kind of a "nightmare decade," the outlook is mixed. On one hand, public money will keep flowing as long as governments have functional currencies to print, which is a short-term positive. But once reality bites and governments are forced to scale back their spending, subsidies for cleantech may be one of the casualties. That is an intermediate-term negative.

Long-term, cleantech's time will come, and the best of technologies and companies in the field will see growing acceptance in the marketplace. Car sales, for instance, soared during the Great Depression because it was time for cars to take over for horses. The same will be true of cleantech once it reaches a point of clear superiority over today's dirtier alternatives.

If someone wanted to be involved in cleantech, three avenues are available:

1) Writing about it. For this, read everything you can get your hands on, and then either begin blogging (very low barriers to entry — I know a dozen people from all walks of life who began posting their ideas online and now make a living at it) or seek out one of the publications that cover the field. Most large newspapers have a tech beat, while online sources such as Greentech Media employ large staffs. None pay well, but they offer experience.

2) Investing in the field. For this you will need either a finance degree or a background in a related scientific field. With one of these in hand, seek out the mutual funds and brokerage houses that specialize in cleantech, and apply for an entry-level job. Bear in mind though that many other would-be clean-tech analysts have the same idea, so the competition is fierce.

3) Working in the field. Get a degree in a related field, materials engineering or something similar and seek out the fastest-growing companies in what you consider the most interesting niches. Here again, competition will be stiff, but growing companies tend to hire large numbers of people, and with the right credentials, you will be well received.

Hydroponics

One of the other ideas being put forward to produce more food is hydroponics, which is a technology for soilless growing that uses nutrients circulated in water tanks. As such, it can be undertaken in many areas, including in cities where there is no suitable land for normal agriculture. This could help solve some problems in two different ways. First, a great deal of the food you find in the grocery store has traveled a long distance and frequently from other countries. It is possible that the amount of locally grown or processed food is only about one-tenth of what you see. There is a popular reaction to this in the form of local farmers markets, but the majority of food is bought from the large chains and consequently bartered in vast quantities with the growers.

The second issue is that of the availability of agricultural land. With increasing population comes a greater demand for housing, and frequently, farmland is sold into developers' hands for them to develop a subdivision. Small farmers are at a tremendous financial disadvantage compared with the giants of the agricultural industry such as ADM, and it is frequently worthwhile for them to sell. This means there is potentially less local food available.

Scientist Dr. Dickson Despommier has been offering a solution to this for a few years and has written a book called *The Vertical Farm: Feeding the World in the 21st Century*, published by Thomas Dunne Books, which explains his ideas. He sees hydroponics, or the growing of plants in water under carefully controlled conditions, as an idea that can solve many problems. There are many advantages to his way of thinking, with a basic notion that crops can be grown locally with multistory indoor hydroponic farming. Some of the advantages include the ability to grow regardless of the weather and with a reduced exposure to pests and disease. The system is efficient; it reuses water that in conventional agriculture would be lost to the ground, and by farming in this way locally, it encourages local labor.

At the time of writing, the system has not been implemented in practice, though Dr. Despommier continues to educate with television and other interviews. So, at present, nothing is investable, but this concept is one that may gain traction in the next few years, and it is interesting to track its progress. Despommier sees this as a method, admittedly hypothetical at this stage, to bring agricultural sustainability to cities. You can find more details at **www.verticalfarm.com**, a website and blog created by Dr. Despommier to outline the news and ideas behind hydroponics.

Fish Farming

As mentioned in the introduction to this chapter, fish stocks are becoming depleted around the world. The UN, in a recent sustainability report, said that more than half of all fish stocks are fully exploited already, one-fifth are over-exploited, and one-twelfth are depleted — only one in five, mostly in the lower-priced sector, are underexploited. Yet, a developing middle class around the world demands more fish at an increasing rate. The position is even worse around the United States, where the U.S. National Oceanic and Atmospheric Administration (NOAA) estimate that a third of fish stocks in coastal waters are already at risk.

This problem almost has sneaked up on us. The fact is that the fishing industry is extremely efficient at large-scale fishing, with so-called factory ships, and unlike growing things on a fixed farm, the oceans are wide open for many different workers to take advantage of them. No one trying to make a profit can be blamed for taking as much as possible, but the result of that will be that there is nothing left for anyone to catch. Chapter 1 talked about peak oil, the time when the maximum amount of oil was being extracted and from which there will be less oil retrieved year after year. The situation in the fishing industry is similar, with "peak fish" already having been achieved. Some projections say that continuing to fish as we are will result in the oceans being "fished out" by 2050.

There is one notable difference however. This only refers to capture fish production, or wild fish. The limits for wild fishing appears to almost reach its limit, with just more than 170 billion tons of fish and shellfish caught every year. Curiously, the fishing industry is still subsidized, and this no doubt adds to the willingness to fish oceanic waters to the maximum. The difference from the oil industry is that there are alternative means of supplying more fish. Aquaculture, or the growing of fish in captivity, has expanded more quickly than any other form of food production and now accounts for about half of the world fish market, compared to just 4 percent in 1970.

The traditional way to fish farm is to raise fish in concrete tanks located near inland sources of water or to grow fish offshore in huge nets for containment. There are problems with both methods of cultivation, but they have been and continue to be used successfully to supply a great deal of the farmed fish. A problem common to both methods is a matter of disease. The fish are grown in close quarters, and this means that diseases spread rapidly and have to be dealt with quickly using antibiotics. If the fish are offshore, there may be consequences for the natural environment. Using inland tanks reduces the possibility of the disease spreading to the wild stock but carries the penalties of large energy usage, continually pumping water through filters to keep the fish healthy. These limitations mean that relying on traditional fish farming to make up the quantities that the world is demanding will result in soaring prices.

Another problem with traditional offshore net farms is that beachfront property tends to be more expensive, which adds to the cost of fish farming. Some companies have been tackling this problem by looking further outward. One solution appears to be to establish fish farms in the open sea using open, often netting, structures where there is no need for pumping water or waste disposal, and the fish are growing in a natural environment. Although this idea has been established for several years, there are still several different solutions, and it appears poised for major expansion as the shortage of fish becomes more evident.

OceanSpar (**www.oceanspar.com**) provides fish pens designed to be moored in the open sea and have a capacity up to nearly 900,000 cubic feet. These fish pens can be moored out at sea, at a depth of up to 100 feet, and can hold tens of thousands of fish. The advantage of mooring them beneath the surface is that even in severe storms the sea will be relatively calm at that depth. All that can be seen is a single marker buoy. Yet, the currents in the open sea will ensure the fish stay healthy and reduce the need for antibiotics. Another system being developed is from Ocean Farm Technologies Inc. (OFT). They have a patented geodesic sphere used for fish containment at sea; this system is being tested by Massachusetts Institute of technology (MIT) researchers off the coast of Puerto Rico. The system uses propellers to slowly move the cage from place to place. OFT (**www.oceanfarmtech.com**) has received a number of grants and private funding for its device, which is called the Aquapod™. Both OceanSpar and Ocean Farm Technologies, Inc., are not yet available to the private investor, but they represent a technology that will no doubt become more important in the future.

Two companies that are using and researching these methods of growing fish are Puerto Rico-based Snapperfarm and Hawaii-based Kona Blue Water Farms (**www.kona-blue.com**). There is ongoing research on the amount of impact such methods may have on the environment, and there are inevitably some objectors to this method. However, it seems that of the options available, offshore ocean farming may prove to be the least harmful. One danger is that genetically engineered fish, designed to grow more rapidly than wild fish, may be used in such containment, and genetic contamination of the wild stock is a possibility. This is similar to other GM products with the hope that any unwanted effects are minimal. The same risk applies for traditional fish farming in nets offshore, and this is a viable industry.

Although the companies mentioned are at present in private hands, there has been extensive research and testing with several universities involved. The companies have received grants and venture capital and may come on the public market in the future provided their pilot schemes are successful. Other areas open to investment include the providers of the nets and materials for the enclosures and fish nurseries who can supply GM fish to stock the enclosures. This is a subject that has great potential in view of the increasing demand for fish, and it seems almost inevitable that some form of fish farming system along these lines must be used in the future.

COMPANIES MENTIONED IN THIS CHAPTER

Monsanto (**www.monsanto.com**)

DuPont (**www.dupont.com**)

Dow Chemical (**www.dow.com**)

Bayer (**www.bayer.com**)

Syngenta (**www.syngenta.com**)

Hain Celestial Group (**www.hain-celestial.com**)

United Natural Foods (**www.unfi.com**)

OceanSpar (**www.oceanspar.com**)

OFT (**www.oceanfarmtech.com**)

Kona Blue Water Farms (**www.kona-blue.com**)

Chapter 12

Pollution and Carbon Trading

Investing in the green movement can include funding or buying shares in clean-tech companies, as well as investing in conventional large companies that have shown an active interest in developing sustainability products and services. There is another way of investing that is directly related to the environment, and that is trading in pollution, or carbon trading. Almost inevitably, if something has value, it will be traded, and the imposition of rules by different national and international entities on the production of carbon dioxide means there is a value to reducing pollution.

Pollution is increasingly a topic addressed by law, typically with the Environmental Protection Agency (EPA) in the U.S., and rightly so, as it protects the health of the country's people. Despite political lobbying, it is likely that restrictions only will become more severe. This means it is now possible to put a monetary value on the rights to emit pollution into the atmosphere. There is already a system in place in Europe, where the cost in early 2011 of 1 ton of carbon dioxide emission was approximately $19. This value depends on supply and demand, and there have been early teething problems establishing a stable market. The price of one carbon allowance plummeted following news in 2006 that several countries had allocated far more credits than were needed for their industries.

Carbon Trading

The European Union Emissions Trading System (EU ETS) was launched in 2005 and is a "cap and trade" system. This simply means there is a limit, or cap, on the total amount of greenhouse gases that can be emitted by a particular company or factory. The emissions are tracked and, at the end of the year, reconciled to the permitted amount. If the company has emitted less than its allowance, it can either keep its spare carbon allowances for future use or trade them to other companies. If the company has emitted more than its allowance, it must trade with other companies to buy allowances to cover its emissions or face hefty fines. Each year, the permitted amount of pollution is reduced in line with regulatory standards. This put a value on taking measures to reduce pollution. The company can either actually reduce pollution or pay money to other companies to buy additional allowances.

The hoped-for result is that profits will make carbon reduction a viable business and ensure many players enter the market and give positive results. But it also has the effect that a company can undertake its own improvements to offset its own older practices. For example, an electrical utility could create a solar farm that would serve to offset pollution from an aging coal-fired generating plant. Cap and trade allows the flexibility to do that rather than try to improve, possibly at high cost, all generating plants to the same efficiencies. The companies are not constrained to reduce emissions across the board and can trade if circumstances require by paying the cost for "carbon credits" from other businesses to avoid renewing a plant that is uneconomic to improve.

The intention is that carbon allowances are reduced over time, and the industry in general will emit less pollution, so the economics in five years may make it viable to upgrade existing practices rather than trading. This overall reduction easily can be accomplished under a cap and trade system by the simple means of the regulating body issuing fewer allowed credits each year. Because it is a trading system with a free-market setting the price, it is up to the companies to apply their best guesses in advance to plug into their cost calculations, so any inordinate costs are passed on to commerce, and in practice, the emissions will be reduced.

Despite the initial problems, which seem to have been associated with an excessive original amount of pollution being permitted, this system has helped reduce overall pollution, and the EU introduced auctioning of allowances in 2013 to make trading easier. Extension of these rules to worldwide pollution can only be a matter of time. The fact that they are not worldwide already is causing some problems, as the European Union is seeking to regulate emissions from international flights and ships that land or dock in the area covered by the EU ETS, and this went into effect in January 2012. U.S. airlines and others are, of course, fighting this hard.

Some commentators feel that a cap-and-trade system suffers the fundamental flaw that it gives offenders the meritorious right to pollute. After all, they are paying for it when they produce excess pollution, so they may not feel such guilt about adding to the problem as they would otherwise. The marketplace can cause temporary problems. For instance, if one year everyone decided not to make reductions in their emissions, the cost of carbon offsets would skyrocket. However, the system encourages users to err on the side of caution, as unused credits can be carried forward and are not forfeited, so, in practice, the system should encourage responsible and excess savings.

Therefore, greenhouse gases effectively have become a commodity to be traded, and the market is growing rapidly. What this means is that companies are set up to find the most financially advantageous projects in which to invest to reduce emissions and obtain carbon credits or offsets. These offsets then can be sold for a profit. The companies that find the most cost-effective projects make the most money.

There are some ways that companies can take better control of their operations and reduce their emissions, often with a reduction in energy expenditure. The most obvious of these is better control of heating and air conditioning, coupled with resetting the thermostats to demand less of the system. The U.S. is particularly bad at emissions, with each American responsible for producing about 19 or 20 tons of carbon dioxide per year, compared with a European average of 10 tons, and 4 tons for each Chinese. Employers can encourage their staff to think twice before printing out e-mail and can order recycled paper, which will help a little.

Changing the type of computer display to a flat panel saves about half of the conventional screen, though laptop computers save even more energy, along with turning computers off when you are not using them. Occupancy sensors that turn off the light and air conditioning can help in an office where the staff is sometimes out on the job. But much more power is consumed in manufacturing, and each type of manufacturing brings its own challenges and solutions.

For maximum success, this requires the trait of thinking outside the conventional markets and seeking worldwide opportunities. Take, for example, the work of Climate Change Capital (**www.climatechangecapital.com**), a private fund based in London that currently manages around €750 million of private capital for various corporate investors, such as pension funds. It has raised capital for many different projects, including making energy from waste in China and Hungary and eliminating industrial gases in China and India. One of its best successes was to seek out a project in China involving the now-superseded refrigerant gas HFC-23. Although this gas is not found in the developed world, it still is used in the emerging markets, and China is a major producer. It is a particularly harmful gas, with global warming effects many thousands of times worse than the same weight of carbon dioxide. Even so, its disposal is relatively simple — it costs 17 euro cents for the equivalent to each ton of carbon dioxide. With the current carbon trading price of around €13 ($19) per ton of CO_2, it is easy to see that this project was bound to be a success.

Natural recipes

Not all carbon reduction has to be done through such tricky manipulations. The balance of the planet has long depended on humans breathing oxygen and expelling carbon dioxide, with plants absorbing the carbon dioxide and returning the oxygen to the atmosphere. Therefore, increasing the amount of planting will reduce the carbon dioxide levels. This provides an alternative, albeit land consuming, way to balance the carbon dioxide emissions. If trees are cut down, then simply by reforestation, the carbon dioxide will be removed again as the young trees grow, restoring the status quo.

Unfortunately, this planet has reached a point where such actions, while laudable and in other ways worthwhile, particularly in terms of restoring the ecosystem of the forest, are not going to make a lot of difference to the greenhouse gases. Reforestation and its sister afforestation, which means planting trees where none existed before, at least in recent times, can only have a limited effect. Afforestation is a part of the Kyoto Protocol, with the belief that forests can act as sinks, soaking up the carbon dioxide, but a recent academic study, published in *Nature*, concludes that even if all the cropland in the world were afforested, it would reduce global warming by less than 1 degree F by 2100. Using just half the cropland for afforestation reduces the temperature by less than one-half of a degree. Even if afforestation was shown to be effective in combating the effects of greenhouse emissions, it is doubtful that even half the cropland could be committed to it, as it would require a doubling of crop yields just to maintain the food supply

Taxes?

Although carbon trading is for companies and countries, this does not mean that steps are not being taken to reduce individual pollution. It is unfashionable to call them taxes, but some places levy an additional charge for heavy pollution, such as associated with large utility vehicles. You have only to think of the taxes accepted on goods such as cigarettes and alcohol to realize that "sin taxes" have a long-standing basis in society. There is a tax on gasoline, and arguably, any fossil fuel or fossil-fuel-generated products should have an additional cost added to balance the cost to society of dealing with the subsequent pollution from burning it.

As may be expected, California is one of the states levying such a charge, and it is called a system benefit charge to avoid the stigma of another tax. The funds promote energy efficiency and education and are used toward rebates. But interestingly, the New York State Public Service Commission (PSC) established such a charge as long ago as 1996. It requires the utility companies to add a percentage to the consumer's bill, which is specifically earmarked for efficiency projects. This has raised nearly $2 billion in that time.

Investing in Carbon Trading

It must be said that this is a sophisticated if young market, and a great deal of research and financial power is going into the carbon marketplace. It is not the place for the fainthearted or the amateur, and it cannot be recommended to the casual investor looking for the "next big thing."

The markets are heavily influenced by government policies of every nation, as these same policies set up the markets and the trading opportunities in the first place. The corporate players in the markets are sophisticated and their knowledge specialized to an extent that is not generally open to the public. The actual expert evaluations of emission reductions are very complex, and even professionals can have problems. Notably, even a professional company such as the Irish-based AgCert™ has run into difficulties.

AgCert is a company that sells carbon offsets to companies by reducing greenhouse gas emissions. It started with a focus on agriculture, as you may guess from the name, and achieved the offsets by capturing and burning methane from animal waste. Agricultural emissions account for about 20 percent of greenhouse gases, and methane is roughly 20 times worse than carbon dioxide, so despite producing carbon dioxide from the burning of methane, the process is still very ecologically advantageous.

Unfortunately, in 2007, the carbon offsets produced were certified by the U.N. to be less than they had anticipated, which left AgCert with a shortfall in its commitment that had to be satisfied from the open market. The result was a plummeting stock price, from a high of 272 pence down to less than a tenth of that. In 2008, AgCert became a subsidiary of the AES Corporation. This goes to show that even the experts can be caught out in this challenging marketplace.

The other problem for the private investor is that the major banks and funds are aggressively pursuing this market, which leaves little space for the private investor to take an interest. However, with the size of the markets being more than $100 billion, you may want to look at some investment. It is a risky marketplace, but you can take part by investing through a fund or specialist trading company. In this way, you will have access to the expertise of professionals who try to keep up with the sector for a living, and give yourself the best chance.

COMPANIES MENTIONED IN THIS CHAPTER

Climate Change Capital (**www.climatechangecapital.com**)

Chapter 13

The Losers

T hankfully, green investing and cleantech are rapidly becoming seen for the necessity they are. This means few companies will not shift their focus in the near future and embrace the principles that have been outlined in this book. In that sense, perhaps there will be no losers but only those who are slower to change, which could result in missing some interim opportunities.

Aside from this, there is no way of knowing just when and how any remaining "dinosaur" companies will see the light and jump on board, so no one will be singled out in this chapter. Even companies which have built their empires around unsustainable practices, as, for example, the oil companies, have widened their original remit and are seeking to become experts in and known for the wider field of energy supply.

That said, this chapter will consider practices that are not sustainable and that would be best abandoned as quickly as possible. Many previous civilizations did not change their ways and, consequently, have passed into history. Although it may seem that such a fate for us would be extreme, now more than ever we have the capability to totally waste our world and suffer the consequences.

Just to emphasize this point, consider one of the most well known of previous civilizations, the Roman Empire. In its heyday, Rome ruled over about 60 million people, back in the days when that was a significant part of the world's population. Nobody thought the regime could end, and it deployed significant numbers of well-trained troops on well-paved roads to ensure the empire thrived and prospered. Agriculture had been developed to a stage where food could be provided to the soldiers, who were freed from the burden of trying to grow crops to feed themselves. What could go wrong?

One of its fundamental problems was the basis on which the Empire developed — capturing new resources to replace those that had been depleted within its previous boundaries, an expansionist development of society not unlike the original colonization of North America. The depletion of resources — using up things that at the time had seemed to be nearly infinite such as trees for construction and as an energy source — contributed to the ultimate downfall of the Empire. This was despite the fact that trees covered most of Europe when the expansion commenced.

The felling of trees was not always considered a problem because the amount of land that needed to be farmed to feed everyone had to be expanded, and this required the clearing of the woods. So it continued, with capturing of new resources becoming more important as the original areas were unable to maintain their way of civilization. In hindsight, it is easy to see that this created a feedback loop that was doomed to fail. Many parallels can be drawn to our twentieth century way of existence.

In fact, in our modern existence it almost has been a principle that the world can be altered by our technology to any extent required for the result, and some people still believe we can engineer our way out of the many legitimate threats that are looming. Unfortunately, with finite resources, that answer cannot prevail.

The Modern Threats

Having asserted that many of our practices are in need of change, it is time to see which should be reduced or avoided, so investments that focus on them can be rejected. First, in energy terms, the fossil fuels have been a steady investment for some time. Shell and BP shares, for example, were for decades considered rock solid and steadily growing in value.

The oil companies are not sitting idly by while cleantech grows, so these and others may do well in the future, but it cannot be based on the original standard practices of drilling, refining, and selling. Even with horizontal drilling giving access to much larger areas of an oil field, and with extraction by different processes from oil shale, only so much oil is available.

M.King Hubbert worked for Shell

Offshore oil rig

and famously made predictions about the amount of oil in the world that could be exploited. He predicted "Hubbert's Peak," or peak oil, as referred to previously. In the middle of the twentieth century, he correctly predicted that the U.S. oil production would peak in 1970, and that global oil production would peak about 2005. Although some have argued with his use of the simple bell curve graph representing the oil output over time, there is little doubt that his theories were correct in principle.

The amount of oil produced from crude in 2005 was about 75 million barrels per day and has declined since then. The overall production, which includes using reserves, biofuels, and other non-crude sources, has been kept steady at about 85 million barrels per day for the time being.

Although these issues affect other countries, particularly in the emerging economies, it is the U.S., in particular, that has grown up with an inherent dependency on cheap energy, with larger automobiles and houses than anyone truly needs becoming the expectation.

One of the ways in which some respondents try to argue with Hubbert's predictions is by pointing out that new ways, such as oil sands and extraction from shale, have been and may continue to be found, leaving the actual "running out of oil" calculation open-ended. What they misunderstand is that Hubbert anticipated that more complex and more energy intensive ways of extracting oil could be invented, and he did not say that all oil would become exhausted. Instead, he took a practical view of the exploitation of it.

In 1982, he said, "There is a different and more fundamental cost that is independent of the monetary price. That is the energy cost of exploration and production. So long as oil is used as a source of energy, when the energy cost of recovering a barrel of oil becomes greater than the energy content of the oil, production will cease no matter what the monetary price may be." In other words, it becomes too energy intensive to extract the oil in relation to the energy that the oil contains.

As goes the oil saga, so goes the natural gas story. At the time of writing, the market in natural gas is surging, and the reasons for this are understandable. It is an alternative fuel that is much cleaner to burn than oil and requires less processing from extraction to end use. Most of the natural gas supplies are sourced right here in the U.S., due in part to the fact that it is more difficult to transport from other countries than oil but also because natural gas supplies are apparently plentiful. On the face of it, natural gas is a viable and plentiful fuel for the future.

To believe in this, however, requires that you suspend your belief in climate-change theories. The world is on record as getting warmer in general, and the pace at which this is happening also is increasing, which demonstrates a feedback loop that increasing temperatures create the circumstances for more increase in temperatures, for example, by melting away the reflective polar ice caps and exposing dark heat-absorbing subsurface layers. Carbon dioxide and other more exotic gas emissions have been blamed for trapping the heat and not allowing it to reradiate into space, and these emissions are increasing with the emerging markets, even if there is no increase in the developed nations. The International Energy Agency foresees that carbon dioxide in the atmosphere will increase by 130 percent before 2050, and no one truly knows what this means in terms of rising sea levels and faltering crops.

So, although some of the issues surrounding oil are not applicable to the natural gas field, the industry cannot deny in the future the underlying global problems caused by using fossil fuels. The earth's natural balance includes carbon dioxide emissions occurring at regular intervals as forests were torched by lightning strikes, but those same forests had previously grown and absorbed an equivalent amount of carbon dioxide. With fossil fuels, the carbon dioxide from the plants that formed the fuel was absorbed eons ago, and to release it now upsets an atmospheric balance that has been stable for millenia.

Carbon dioxide levels now have increased to a level not seen since at least 650,000 years ago. A European study which looked at the ice of Antarctica in 2004 drilled about 2 miles down, the equivalent of looking back in time 900,000 years. They found that the current carbon dioxide levels are actually about 30 percent higher than at any previous time. This has been borne out by a U.S. study that reached the same conclusion at the end of 2007 from annual measurements taken on one of Hawaii's volcanoes, and concluded that this was due mainly to the burning of coal, oil, and natural gas. So, let it not be thought that fossil fuels, however "clean" the combustion, are a long-term solution.

Among the real losers in the sustainable future when climate change will become increasingly important, you should include any high intensity carbon-using companies, such as forestry, livestock farming, and mining, except to the extent that they can change their practices. You also must watch out for the less intense carbon industries, such as tourism, which may be negatively impacted.

Industries that are known carbon emitters are bound over time to suffer increasing regulation as governments try to limit their impact, and one of the tools likely to be used is higher taxation, providing a disincentive and affecting profits. Mining, although in some areas needed for the materials to supply cleantech, will be hit by greater pollution controls as well as by rising energy costs.

Forestry suffers because there is a need to retain more trees and not use them for paper and other products, and hence paper industries may feel the impact. Livestock farming can suffer on several counts — livestock produces methane gas, which a United Nations report puts at the equivalent of 18 percent of the carbon dioxide emissions; and the dwindling resources, such as water supplies and food, will make meat more expensive and a less cost-effective way of producing protein for human consumption than many others.

Finally, it may not be a rosy future for the insurance industry. As climate events become more extreme, as it seems they are already starting to do, there will be increasing risks that the industry standards are not familiar with accounting for. In a competitive industry, the first companies to raise rates may lose out, but those who do not might find themselves without any profits. Even the increased risks of massive forest fires can impact housing insurance.

Taking the Real Overview

As you have seen, there are issues with the image that some companies try to convey and with the reality. As with all marketing and advertising, the public relations departments of the companies concerned are only trying to portray their image in the best light, but this means you must be alert and understand what underlies corporate actions. For instance, at the time of writing, there is a confidently presented oil company advertisement that emphasizes two points that are implicitly important — amount of reserves and security of supply — and meets these issues by an "engineer" assuring the camera that oil sands are available within the North American continent that contain enough oil for independence of supply from other countries for years to come. What is not stated is that extraction of oil from oil sands requires much more energy, increasing the costs, and that is one reason they are not fully exploited right now. It is more cost effective and competitive to import oil, rather than choose a course that would give no dependency on countries subject to political unrest or action but would make the product more expensive and uncompetitive with other oil companies. Second, oil sands extraction will only exacerbate greenhouse gas emissions, which is noticeably missing from the upbeat advertisement. In other words, to pursue the oil sands option will hasten the deleterious effects of climate change.

Although climate change is a major focus of sustainability, many other issues may concern the green investor. Depletion of the world's resources is inevitable as more demands are placed on them, and it can become a matter of deciding which will run out, in economic terms if not in fact, sooner than another substitute. With the demands placed on natural resources, particularly by developing and emerging economies such as the "BRIC" countries — Brazil, Russia, India, and China — that are experiencing industrial growth and an increasing demand for better goods and services at a moment in history when the planet is least able to supply sufficient raw materials, sustainability of materials consumed in the manufacturing process becomes a primary concern.

The information explosion with the Internet and all its various forms of outlet such as Youtube, Facebook, and Twitter means that companies are less likely to be able to confuse the informed investor. Although it is true that there are many different views expressed on the Internet, some of which are not sustained by facts, on balance the Internet is a resource that used with care provides greater transparency and better information for financial decisions.

It should not be forgotten that regardless of any morality or profit issues, there are powers that can mandate certain company actions. In its most obvious form, this comes from governmental regulation which increasingly will need to restrain unacceptable or unreasonable practices, despite various temporary political moves apparently inspired by lobbyists to release companies from such suppression. If regulation fails to control harmful actions, there is the prospect of growing pressure from international non-governmental organizations ((NGOs) to replace that protective mantle with public concern, which will still achieve the result of failing performance for companies that have an aversion to changing. Although it may take a little longer than imposing laws would do, in the long run, the losing companies will underperform and fail or be forced to change.

Chapter 14

Looking Ahead

t is truly difficult to decide what to include in this chapter. So much of the cleantech discussed earlier is, by its very nature, looking ahead, with designs that are still to come to market or that can be further exploited in the fullness of time that to anticipate further into the future requires a measure of psychic ability.

That said, a couple of ideas are at present more of a gleam in the eye than viable projects, and these would qualify as potential, though by no means proven, concepts that might be of major consequence in the more distant future.

Fusion

Mention nuclear power and the immediate reaction is likely to point to the accidents that can happen, evidenced most recently by the Fukushima nuclear disaster caused by an earthquake on March 11, 2011. As mentioned in Chapter 3, conventional nuclear power is not green, even if it is seen by some as a convenient stopgap source of energy in the face of other energy issues. But fusion is a different type of nuclear power, and though it may be some decades away from practical implementation, it has significant benefits in comparison.

Conventional nuclear power is a fission process, which means that atoms are split and release strong forces. Most energy sources are chemical processes that release energy. Burning any type of fuel is a chemical combination with oxygen (O), so that carbon (C) combines to produce carbon dioxide (CO_2) and hydrogen (H) combines to make water (H_2O), for example. Depending on the chemical combination, it either requires energy or gives up energy when chemical combining takes place, and in these particular cases, energy in the form of heat is released or given up.

Nuclear power can unleash energy on a totally different level, millions of times more powerfully. It is based on taking apart or combining the components of atoms, and this is why nuclear bombs can release so much energy from a comparatively small device. The type of nuclear power used in current reactors is fission, which means it involves splitting atoms to get energy. This type of power has to be carefully controlled with cooling water and complex safeguards to keep it from running away and multiplying uncontrollably, called a chain reaction, as in a bomb. The reason it could do this, in basic terms, is that the reaction is initiated by firing a neutron (which is part of an atom) into the nuclear fuel. The response of the fuel to this is to split or breakdown into smaller atoms, and this generates more neutrons in the process, which could lead to a rapid increase in the reaction.

Nuclear fusion, largely theoretical now, is the opposite. It involves taking many small atoms and combining or fusing them together in the process. Now, you do not get anything for nothing, so this reaction can need energy input. If, in theory, you could take the products of a nuclear power plant and recombine them to make the original fuel, uranium, then you would need to add the amount of energy that was previously released. Fission releases energy when large atoms such as uranium are split, but fusion releases energy from combining small atoms. When you fuse together atoms that have a low mass, such as hydrogen and others, they yield energy in the process. One of the most well-known examples of the power of fusion is our sun, and other stars, as fusion is what causes it to give off light and heat. As fusion only happens when you are inputting energy, for example by using lasers, it is inherently far safer than fission and not subject to run-away reactions. If anything goes wrong, it is far more likely to shut down than explode.

Once a stable fusion reaction can be established, producing energy that is effectively cheap heat, then proven processes can be applied to create electricity. The energy most likely would be used to produce steam that would be applied to a steam turbine. The waste products would still be radioactive, as with the existing methods of nuclear power generation, but they would be different materials and ones that would lose their radioactivity in a matter of years, much more quickly than the current waste.

There has been activity for decades researching ways nuclear fusion can be made to perform meaningful work. The hydrogen bomb was an early example of nuclear fusion; Edward Teller developed it in 1952. But useful fusion has focused on the "tokamak" form of reactor, first tried by the Soviet Union in the 1960s and still being actively applied today. The tokamak requires a doughnut-shaped containment field for the fusion plasma, which is maintained by a magnetic field.

In the UK, fusion experiments have been taking place since the 1980s in Oxfordshire. The details of the experiments have some amazing figures. For instance, in 2008, a laser was used to heat matter up to ten million degrees centigrade (about 18 million degrees Fahrenheit) for a tiny fraction of one second, actually just one-trillionth. Although a lot was learned, it is still only one-tenth of the temperature required for nuclear fusion at the pressures we have on Earth, but the scientists are learning all the time. Lasers have superseded the previous methods used, which included superconducting magnets.

Other experimental installations are being built, codenamed ITER, IGNITOR and in California the NIF (National Ignition Facility). There are many obstacles, some of which detractors feel would need miracles to overcome. For instance, the extremely high temperatures are only sustainable if they can be contained by the design, yet there is no way to generate the temperatures except by working fusion reactors, so no easy method exists to develop the expertise ahead of time. The fuels used are heavier forms of hydrogen, called deuterium and tritium. Deuterium is apparently no problem; it is found in copious amounts in seawater, but only twenty kilograms of tritium are known to exist in the world. It is estimated that a typical working fusion reactor would burn about 50 kilograms of tritium per year. Add to this the fact that tritium costs about $30 million per kilogram, and the problems seem insurmountable.

The answer scientists tell us is that a fusion reactor can produce more tritium as part of its operation. It would become self-sustaining, breeding its own fuel supply. The technology exists in theory, but this has never been demonstrated, and the disbelievers say that a reactor would need to operate for several months before it achieved the stability needed to produce the fuel.

Nonetheless, many proponents think that all problems can be faced and overcome in time, and there is active research now into nuclear fusion as a source of power. This is taking place both on a small scale private venture capital way and with large government-funded activities, and there is no one clear method that stands out for success. The race to solve the issues and produce a commercially viable form of fusion power after 50 years of experimentation is still not decided between big government-funded projects and small startup companies.

One of the small companies trying to find a future in fusion is called Helion Energy (**www.helionenergy.com**), based in Washington. They have taken a different approach to the tokamak, with a pulsed design where two clouds of gas collide inside a burn chamber, releasing extreme heat. This makes it relatively compact, and more important for venture capital investors, cheap. This does not mean that investment companies are flocking to the door, as there are still admittedly many problems to face before any commercial design can be made, but it represents an alternative that could come to market at some time and gives hope for private industry. This is not investable for several if not many years, but looking ahead could prove one of the best answers to the energy crisis.

CASE STUDY:
DOING WHAT FEELS RIGHT

Renee Morgan, MA
President
Better World Investments, Inc.
1165 Odyssey Court
Lafayette, CO 80026
720-890-6106 or 800-990-6206
www.betterworldinvestments.com

My education consists of a BA in political science and a MA in counseling psychology. Although this may be an odd entry into financial planning, it probably makes apparent my interest in socially responsible investing. After many years of service in the public sector, I entered the private sector and have been in the financial services industry for 11 years. I remain passionate about politics and service to the nonprofit world and continue to participate whenever I can. After working in a corporate environment for four years, I started my own company seven years ago. I use National Planning Corporation as my broker dealer, one of the largest independent b/ds in the business.

I got involved with investing somewhat arbitrarily. I was a counselor at a detox center and knew I wanted to leave the counseling world. I had been involved with grant writing and fund-raising in the nonprofit world for years, so money and how money works was not all together new, but the stock market was. I answered an ad and jumped in; it was not the most thoughtful process. As far as green investing, the area I live in and the people I know asked almost immediately if I was doing it, so I looked into it. It was so clearly the only way I could feel good about the work I do that I jumped in, pretty much as a lone wolf in a corporation that thought I was crazy.

I did not have a financial background. I had an education and work experience in both politics and nonprofits, so my exposure to money was in grant writing and fund-raising. I learned the technical aspect of the business; i.e. how stocks and bonds work, retirement planning, savings structures, IRS codes at the corporation that hired me. However, I believe my counseling background has helped immensely in establishing and maintaining strong relationships with my clients. Of course, a huge dose of honesty also helps.

The most interesting part of green investing is the impact is has. Through proxy voting and behind the scenes negotiations, real change happens that directly impacts people's lives and the world we live in. Most computer parts are recyclable now largely due to SRI (socially responsible investing); old growth trees are not used for lumber largely due to SRI; children have been put back into school and pulled out of fields due to SRI. The list goes on and on, but it is the reason I do SRI. Also, through community investing, people all over the world are able to better their lives directly. They start businesses, buy cows, and have cleaner drinking water, mosquito nets, and housing.

The biggest problem in the SRI field is the watering down of what we do. As SRI gains in momentum and popularity, many people claim to do it who really do not. They know of a few mutual funds, but they do not understand proxy voting or community investing. Screened investments are just a tiny bit of what the overall SRI is. Even worse are financial planners who say they are SRI or investments that claim to be green and simply are not. It is very confusing to the consumer who wants green investments but is being led astray. It is a bit like clean coal. There is no such thing as clean coal, but the coal industry wants people to believe there is.

In terms of the recent downturn in markets and global recession, my job has not changed at all. I help individuals reach their financial goals. Investing in the stock market should be one part of that plan. It is the part I know quite a bit about. The world is an uncertain and a topsy-turvy place. As long as people are diversified properly and not chasing the next big thing, they will fare OK. My clients were not overly hurt in the downturn of 2008 to 2009. It is about planning and being reasonable about expectations. SRI can help protect against some of this. As far as executive compensation, my clients never owned several companies because of excessive executive compensation. Companies that have unfair practices tend to also be the ones with problems in other areas.

I have certain qualities that made it imperative for me to work in green investing. The primary reason is a serious sense of justice and doing what feels right. I could not work for my own personal income alone. My entire background and interest is in helping people and striving for a better world. It only made sense that I do that using money instead of directly helping in a therapeutic setting or on a political campaign. Also, I genuinely like people, so a real interest in my clients' lives and well-being has proved vital.

One of my biggest challenges was becoming adept at working with money and understanding that wealth can be used for social justice. In fact, at this point, I believe it has far greater impact than any street protest. But I did not start out believing that.

This is an extraordinarily difficult field to get into. If I have advice for someone looking to break into it, I would say get used to being broke for a few years. Eventually, you get to work where and how you want, but it takes a tremendous amount of perseverance. It is fantastic work, but for now, there is no easy way in. Most people start at the traditional firms, learn the business, and then break out on their own after a bit.

Wind Developments

The chapter on wind power detailed the different ways in which wind turbines have developed and are being used, with tried technology being refined with advanced materials, blade profiles, and other tweaks. Looking a little further ahead, there are a batch of ideas, called airborne wind turbines, which are seeking to open up a different direction for wind power.

As the name suggests, this set of solutions have in common the idea that the power generation from wind can be made less obtrusive and more reliable by using the winds that blow steadily a thousand feet or higher in the sky. Unlike conventional wind turbines, the devices would not have towers for support, but fly, perhaps like kites, although there are several different approaches.

If the technology can be developed — and no one has yet produced a commercial prototype, even though some have experimental models — then it is estimated that airborne wind turbines could supply 10 percent of the planet's electricity requirements. The advantages are a high yield of consistent power in comparison to the earthbound wind turbines that are already in use, and the power production is clean and virtually free once the devices are in service. It is projected that the turbines could fly for approximately 80 to 95 percent of the time between maintenance stops, and this means a much higher production than ground-based wind turbines, which typically only can output an average of about 30 percent of their rated capacity due to varying conditions.

The problems to be overcome are not simply devising the best mechanical systems to generate power in flight but also formulating ways in which the devices can be flown safely, with any failures not resulting in the turbine crashing to the ground but being gently recovered. As they would not be manned flying vehicles, at least not in the current incarnations, there should be no on-board pilots to endanger. One answer might be to fly them only over uninhabitable areas or offshore, but at the same time, the industry does not need self-destroying failures, particularly when forensic examination might be needed to discover the reason for the failure.

Types of airborne turbines

The airborne turbines can take many different forms, each with its own advantages and challenges. The general concept is that the machine is tethered to the ground, using the tether as a means to transmit the electricity produced, but there the similarities end. Many of them are designed to swoop around using crosscurrent movement to increase the effective speed of airflow and hence the output. They are not made to sit steadily aloft, except as needed to avoid collisions when wind turbine farms are deployed in the future.

The airborne turbines can be broken down into various configurations. Some are like kites or airplanes, relying on the wind to keep them aloft, and others use a lighter-than-air concept with gas-filled balloons to keep in the air. The balloon has an obvious advantage when it comes to reassuring the public that the device will not readily crash. The other major choice is whether the generator is on the craft or if it is ground mounted with the airborne generator providing the mechanical work through its tether.

One company that appears to be slightly ahead of the crowd is Sky Wind-Power (**www.skywindpower.com**). They have concentrated on what may be called a rotorcraft, which uses four horizontal rotors (like helicopter rotors) to both rise aloft and to generate power. A prototype was flown, and a 1-megawatt version was anticipated in a couple of years. However, there is no airborne turbine in operation at the moment. The operation is straightforward in concept. The rotorcraft flies to the required altitude, at which the tether is taut, by powering the rotors to produce lift. When in place, the attitude or tilt of the craft can be controlled to allow the prevailing wind to maintain the craft aloft and spin the rotors to generate power.

The angle is continuously monitored, both ensuring there is sufficient lift and control of the power produced, should the wind speed increase too far. The company is still privately owned.

Joby Energy (**www.jobyenergy.com**) is another airborne wind pioneer company leading the field, and it is based in California. Unlike Sky Wind-Power, it has a prototype concept that uses multiple propellers and an airframe. From some angles, it looks like a flying wing. It shares the same idea of using the propellers to launch the device and switching over to generating power with them when at altitude. The propellers are driven by and drive motor generators. There are many more propellers than Sky WindPower uses, giving a substantial backup capacity should any fail, and the Joby wind generator is designed to swing around in loops to increase the wind effect. The wings allow for more control of the flight path. There is an explanatory video on the website. The projected size of the airborne generator is around 200 feet wingspan.

Makani Power (**www.makanipower.com**) is another California company experimenting with tethered wind power generators. Its offerings look similar to a glider and have from two to six propeller rotors mounted on the wing for power generation. This company has attracted funding from Google founders as well as government grants. Its operation is similar to Joby Energy's but with the different shape of vehicle. Again the generator is designed and controlled to circle on the tether to increase the apparent wind speed and output, and once more the power generated is transmitted to the ground anchor down the tethering line. The wingspan will be about 120 feet.

An alternative method of power generation is being researched at Ampyx Power (**www.ampyxpower.com**). This company is based in the Netherlands. Although the machine looks similar to the previous generators, it has a different form of generation. The flying part of the installation is a tethered unmanned sailplane, which they call a PowerPlane. This flies in a pattern downwind of the ground anchor, and the tether is allowed to reel out, turning a drum at the ground station to generate electricity. When the tether is fully reeled out, then the plane is made to dive toward the ground base to slacken the tension; the tether is reeled in using much less force, and, hence, power than was obtained on the outward journey. The process then repeats indefinitely. Ampyx has flown a prototype, and Dutch authorities have recognized it as a special category of unmanned aircraft.

For a completely different concept, and just to show how many contrasting variations are being researched in this emergent industry, we need to consider Magenn Power (**www.magenn.com**), based in Washington and Ottawa, a private Canadian corporation. The design, which they claim is a development of their 31 years experience in airship work, is a horizontal cylinder filled with helium and about 60 feet long and 30 feet diameter that is projected to produce about 10 KW of power — not really sufficient for a commercial application but proof of the design. The electricity is generated by the cylinder rolling about a horizontal axis, which it does because there are a series of fins on the surface set at an angle to the wind.

There is a certain beautiful laziness to this operation, contrasting to the swooping of the pseudo airplanes of other manufacturers. The fact that the helium keeps the unit afloat means it is perceived as more acceptable, traditional, and inherently safer than alternatives. Although reassurances can be made to allay fears about the result if, for example, a tether should break on the other designs, the long-standing lighter-than-air concept has an intrinsic head start.

An alternative approach to the lighter-than-air concept is being researched by Altaeros Energies (**www.altaerosenergies.com**), a young company formed by MIT and Harvard alumni with a patented design. They propose what is called a shroud, a helium-filled doughnut on its side, which would have a propeller or rotor in the "hole," generating power. The shape of the ring forces air through, increasing the output.

Although these are all startup companies struggling to devise the best methods of generating power with airborne devices, there also may be some established companies looking at the profit potential. For instance, Honeywell engineers said they had designed a 2-megawatt flying wind turbine based on their expertise designing unmanned drones for military use. They announced this at an airborne wind energy conference in 2010, and apparently, all the parts are available to build it. Curiously, if this is the case, they are not putting it in production and simply have a computer simulation to prove the design. Apparently, one of the reasons for not proceeding is that the market has not yet become real, and that means the shareholders would be unhappy with Honeywell spending time and money advancing the idea any further. However, for Honeywell to have taken the design to this stage must mean they see the potential.

Apart from deciding on the most cost-effective design, pioneers of airborne wind turbines face other problems. Safety must be paramount; as one of the advantages of the high-flying designs is that they are not restricted in location of deployment in the same way that ground-based wind turbines are. There are high winds at altitude over most of the earth, and you have only to consider the difference in flying times for East to West flights compared to West to East to realize the winds can be considered fairly steady and constant. So, a design that is judged dangerous in failure mode and must be used in deserted areas could be at a disadvantage.

Even so, there may be short, relatively calm periods, and this means that a measure of storage or backup power is required, even if not to the extent of traditional wind generators and solar power. Airborne wind generators will benefit from the current work being done in this field, which may come up with the best answers by the time airborne technology is ready for application. In a related context, there also can be severe conditions such as thunderstorms, hurricanes, and tornadoes, which will require the generators to be grounded for safety.

Another less obvious problem is that of birds running into the units. Even for ground-based wind turbines, there can be significant issues with flocks of birds running into the equipment, damaging moving rotors and harming the birds. This occurs particularly when the locations are on major migratory routes. There is no easy answer for this problem, but scientists are working on early detection so impending collisions can be recognized and allowed for. The helium solutions would seem to be a friendlier form of airborne generator in this respect.

Finally, there obviously will need to be work done in conjunction with the Federal Aviation Authority (FAA) and similar bodies in other countries to figure out how these flying objects can merge safely with existing piloted air traffic and perhaps also future unmanned commercial flights. With flexibility of placement, this may be something as simple as marking a "no-commercial-flight" zone on a map for the generators to use. As none of the airborne generators is planned to be more than a couple of thousand feet high, the conflicts mainly would be with low flying private planes and commercial takeoffs and landings, so once there is viable technology, this aspect is something that can be fixed.

Regarding investment opportunities, this realm is in a wait-and-see stage. Venture capital and government grants are providing the seed for research into viable options, and the companies concerned are held largely privately at this time. None of them has been able to provide an autonomous operational flight even of their prototypes, and the best still need a manual pilot for the takeoff and landing phases. If one or two concepts start to dominate and come to the public's attention, then watch for the initial public offerings when the stocks will start to be traded on the markets.

Solar Fuels

Another concept, which is little more than an idea now, is the production of fuels directly from sunlight. This is not as far-fetched as it may sound, as plants routinely create fuels such as wood by a process of photosynthesis, As previously mentioned, this absorbs carbon dioxide while the plant is growing, so when the fuel is burned there is no net increase in global warming gases.

Certainly, we have the technology to produce solar power directly while the sun is shining, but this has the associated problem of storing the power, for example in batteries, until it is needed. Creating fuel would get around the need for developing such storage systems. The question is whether technology can be developed to manufacture fuel directly from sunlight. The process of photosynthesis is being studied with the help of a five-year grant from the U.S. Department of Energy (DOE), with the goal of artificially recreating the process.

The grant, which may extend to $122 million, is going to a Caltech multidisciplinary group, which is known as JCAP — Joint Center for Artificial Photosynthesis (**www.solarfuelshub.org**). The idea is that drawing in many disciplines will spark innovation and make finding solutions more likely. There are several different aspects to photosynthesis, and each has a critical role.

In the State of the Union address in 2011, President Obama referred to this research, saying that the team was developing a way to take carbon dioxide, water, and sunlight to make fuel for cars. It is a long way from the practical stage, but the scientists believe they can produce fuel ten times more efficiently than nature. It is not clear what efficiency means in this case, as nature produces fuel without man's intervention, and certainly without requiring energy input from outside, but possibly it is referring to trying to speed up the process.

It may be thought that ways exist already to generate fuel in the form of hydrocarbons from carbon dioxide and water. However, the project is seeking a direct way, not, for example, by using electrolysis to separate water into its component gases and other known devices. The mission as detailed on the website is to "develop and demonstrate a manufacturable solar-fuels generator, made of Earth-abundant elements, that will take sunlight, water and carbon dioxide as inputs and robustly produce fuel from the sun 10 times more efficiently than typical current crops."

The processes needed so the action of chlorophyll can be emulated require finding catalysts, or substances that facilitate reactions without being changed by them, and those catalysts must be readily available. A substance that has been used as a catalyst for various reactions is platinum, but this cannot be part of the answer for solar fuel, as it is expensive and relatively scarce.

There are several issues to be overcome, summed up as cost, efficiency, and robustness to continue reliably under arduous conditions. Although various processes can deal with some of these aspects, it is not yet obvious how all these attributes may be combined. Several tasks have to be performed, including capturing the light to facilitate the catalytic reactions of splitting the water atoms and combining the hydrogen this yields with carbon dioxide to make hydrocarbon fuel. When the water is broken down into hydrogen and oxygen, these gases must be separated by a membrane to prevent them simply recombining. As previously mentioned, the overall process could be achieved indirectly by making electricity and using other known reactions, but the purpose of the research is to find a way to directly replace photosynthesis and to achieve the effect in real time.

The way that the task is turning out; two catalysts will be needed — one to split the water and the other to make the hydrocarbon fuel. Platinum is out on cost grounds, but a viable substitute is being developed at MIT, although no details have been made available.

There is more research taking place in New Zealand, where a team at Massey University is developing solar cells based on titanium oxide rather than the currently conventional silicon. There may be a significant cost advantage to these, and if they are as good as claimed, they may form the basis of the needed catalyst. At this time, there is no place for the private investor, but this technology could have enormous potential if developed.

 COMPANIES MENTIONED IN THIS CHAPTER

Helion Energy (**www.helionenergy.com**)
Sky WindPower (**www.skywindpower.com**)
Joby Energy (**www.jobyenergy.com**)
Makani Power (**www.makanipower.com**)
Ampyx Power (**www.ampyxpower.com**)
Magenn Power (**www.magenn.com**)
Altaeros Energies (**www.altaerosenergies.com**)

Chapter 15

What You Can Do

H aving read this book, you may feel motivated to not only invest your capital in green investments but also to take steps personally to reduce your carbon footprint. These are not mutually exclusive concepts. You may have heard of Peter Lynch, an investor who is currently a research consultant at Fidelity Investments. He famously has said that you should "invest in what you know."

In his conversations, Warren Buffett constantly emphasizes the "circle of competence," which means all the businesses with which the investor is familiar and completely understands. One of Buffett's investing rules is that if you do not understand a business, you should not invest in it. For instance, if you do not know about fishing lures, it may not make sense to invest in a company that makes them, even if the fundamentals look attractive. Therefore, it makes perfect sense for you to take home some clean-tech products if you are expanding your portfolio to include clean-tech companies.

If you are interested in adopting a greener way of existence, there are many books that can help you decide what measures you can take personally to minimize your current impact on the earth. Atlantic Publishing, for instance, lists *Green Your Home: The Complete Guide to Making Your New or Existing Home Environmentally Healthy*. But such books provide much more than advice related to the companies that make green products. Many green practices are little or no cost; they involve changing habits or use existing products in a more environmental way.

However, there is a counter argument to embracing literally the products you use as the major part of your portfolio, and it involves rational thought. Even if you are delighted with the products and regard the company as well run with good fundamentals, the specter of diversification sometimes is raised. For instance, if you know everything there is to know about outboard motors, this does not mean that your portfolio should be mainly outboard motor manufacturers, albeit the ones that you will

know from your expertise will perform the best. Market sectors go through cycles, and therefore, you should diversify holdings if you want to protect your funds.

Making sure you include many different market sectors in your portfolio can be allay this concern. Even that is not necessarily going to help in the event of a major market move, so you also need to research asset allocation, which is a stage beyond diversification as it looks at investing in different financial instruments that are not correlated in their moves or may even be negatively correlated. These are topics worthy of further study.

Even with the best of intentions, if you try to change your way of life too quickly, you are likely to revert. It is far better to make small changes and assimilate them one at a time before going on to the next. If you decide to alter your lifestyle, you are more likely to stick with it if you only do it incrementally. You also need to be convinced the change is worthwhile; otherwise, there is little incentive to continue. Above all, train yourself to recognize opportunities, and do not be content to be told without evidence how great they are. Remember that many people are too eager to tell you what you want to hear, and some practices certainly do not give you or the environment the benefits they claim.

Your house: Before you do anything more on your house, you need to get an energy audit by an approved contractor. Some utility companies and public bodies will help with the cost, but looking into that is the only possible excuse for delay. The energy audit will give you a baseline from which to plan the most cost-effective and green improvements.

Saving energy: The first step for many properties is to improve the insulation, and the difficulty of doing this depends on what has been found. It comes as no surprise that most homes need more insulation. The cost of insulation does not rise at the same rate as the cost of energy, so what was an economic amount just a few years ago can now be upgraded with financial justification. Most insulation is produced in relatively green ways nowadays, for example, using recycled cellulose (based around used paper), and this can be blown into roofs or walls relatively easily.

Another recommendation will be to change your light bulbs. There are some issues surrounding the green alternatives, particularly the greater first cost, but this will come down over time and, in any case, you shortly will have no alternative available.

If your air-conditioning unit is a few years old, the chances are that it is much less efficient than the current models. This does not necessarily mean it is a good target for replacement, as many people assume and installers will tell you. There are many factors to assess. Each new air-conditioning unit requires a lot of energy and materials to produce, and this is generally reflected in the price. It actually can be kinder to the planet to retain the old unit and use more energy to operate it, rather than accounting for more than this energy in one go when a new unit is made. But you will not find many commercials pointing out this rather obvious fact. You owe it to yourself and the planet to take an overall stance. Nevertheless, you also have to account for the loss of efficiency in a unit that is now oversized because of all the insulation you have done.

Making energy: Making energy is one of the most interesting aspects of what you can do at home. The government passed a law that requires your local utility company to buy surplus energy from you at the price they charge customers for it. In the past, they bought electricity, if they did not have their own generation or the current amount was insufficient, at wholesale rates that were much less, and they resold it to consumers to make a profit. Under the new net metering rules, the utility company is at a disadvantage because they still have to be able to supply the full load on the grid when it is needed, but customers with their own generation will have their bills eased considerably, which reduces revenue.

There are many financial incentives to buying green power generators such as solar panels and wind turbines, which mean the payback period can be reasonable, and as the technology becomes cheaper, there will a swing in favor of making your own power. If you had a house that was "off the grid" with no utility connection, your solar power installation would include significant extra cost for energy storage, with expensive deep-cycle batteries that have a life of about eight years. What net metering means is that the utility company has to provide "virtual batteries" of unlimited size that you automatically use when you generate excess power. This is a great deal for the consumer and will allow you to assess the type of products you can invest in.

Other ways to reduce your home's impact

Saving and making energy are not the only ways that you personally can make a difference. It just demands that you question yourself on each aspect of your life.

Water consumption: This is typically cast as turning off the water when brushing your teeth or shaving, and the choice of appliances, particularly your washing machine, can have a large effect. But you should not forget such items as having a garden that does not need much watering, and using a drip watering system if necessary, rather than sprinklers. Atlantic Publishing has a book, *The Complete Guide to Water Storage: How to Use Gray Water and Rainwater Systems, Rain Barrels, Tanks, and Other Water Storage Techniques for Household and Emergency Use*, that goes into detail on every aspect of water storage and use.

Groceries: Consider buying more locally produced food, as this not only supports your neighbors' businesses, but also reduces the transport costs and may mean fresher produce. If you change your eating habits to feast on foods further down the food chain, you will avoid supporting the system that requires so much corn and water just to produce red meat. A typical vegan diet contributes 1 ½ fewer tons of carbon dioxide equivalent to the atmosphere each year compared to the normal North American diet, according to a study by the University of Chicago. There is probably no need for you to buy expensive bottled water either, as water from the faucet is usually just as good and can be filtered if you want. Plastic bottles that are used for bottled water only add to the problem.

Family transportation: You could decide to keep and repair your car rather than buying a hybrid or electric car. The amount of energy used to make a car is reflected to some extent in its price, so you are not helping the environment if you keep replacing your car every couple of years, even if the newer models run more efficiently. It is a complex calculation, but one worth bearing in mind rather than automatically thinking that you should get the latest, most fuel-efficient vehicle.

Many other little things we do add up to a lot of environmental impact. You may think that using a microwave is efficient, as you are typically only heating or cooking foods for a short time, and not heating the kitchen much. But when you add up the additional impact of the preparation of the typical microwave dinner, including freezing it, transporting it, and keeping it frozen until needed, the actual global impact is significantly higher than just preparing and eating fresh food.

Your work: Depending on your type of employment, many of the new products and technologies could be applicable to your work, and by demonstrating socially conscious thinking and identifying economies you could find that you are looked on in a more favorable light by your employer. Many companies require that networked office computers are kept turned on overnight, which allow for automatic updating of programs and virus checking, but it may be agreeable for them to be shutdown on certain evenings and weekends. If this policy became popular across the country, there would be a noticeable saving in energy usage.

The commute: Many of the things discussed in Chapter 10 on transportation may be applicable to your commute. If you are not able or prepared to change your mode of transport, you can at least make sure you drive economically and leave the house five minutes early so you do not have to rush and use more fuel. If your employer agrees, you might consider staggering your work times to avoid the worst of the traffic, and that will save fuel.

More drastic measures include bicycling to work, and in this regard, you may have to persuade your employer to install a shower for staff use, so you can work comfortably once you get there.

Your time off: It is in the realm of time off that you are free to explore greener exploits. No one is seeking to deprive you of your hobbies, but with a little thought, they might perhaps be realized in ways that are more sustainable. With the increasing costs of travel, many are considering alternative vacation styles that do not need to cause so much carbon dioxide. In general, the U.S. populace is sadly lacking in an awareness of its polluting lifestyle, whereas in Europe it has become popular to have knowledge of one's personal "carbon footprint." Although we are not the leaders in this respect, it would take little to catch up, and change is inevitable. By reducing your thinking to the simple basics, it should become plain where improvements can be made, and it is up to you to make them. If the changes involve cleantech, so much the better, as you can use them to test your investment portfolio.

Conclusion

I t is my hope that in addition to giving you pointers toward a profitable approach to green investing, you also have started to think about every aspect of your life. We do not live in isolation and cannot ignore our personal impact on the world when mankind has proven to be so destructive over time. The financial side is only one part of living, and while I wish you every success in that, any amount of money in a world that is deteriorating around us is, I contend, an ultimately futile goal. I look forward to everyone developing an awareness that will lead us to a better future.

Appendix A

These lists are only starting points for more research. They are here as references and examples of possible investable companies within each field. The companies named are not recommended or endorsed by *Atlantic Publishing*. Make sure to do your own research into whether you want to invest in any of them.

Green Funds:

Acuity Clean Environment Equity (ACUITYCLEANE.TO)

Alger Green Fund (SPEGX)

Appleseed Fund (APPLX)

Calvert Global Alternative Energy (CGAEX)

Calvert Global Water Fund (CFWAX)

Calvert International Equity (CWGVX)

Calvert International Opportunities (CWVYX)

Calvert Large Cap Growth (CLGAX)

Calvert Moderate Allocation (CMAAX)

Calvert Small Cap Fund (CCVAX)

Calvert Social Index (CSXAX)

Claymore S&P Global Water Index (ETF:CWWA:TO)

CRA Qualified Investment (CRATX)

Domini International Social Equity (DOMAX)

Domini Social Equity (DSEPX)

ESG Managers Aggressive Growth Portfolio (PAGAX)

First Trust NASDAQ Clean Edge US (ETF: QCLN)

First Trust ISE Water Index Fund (ETF: FIW)

Gabelli SRI Green mutual fund (SRIAX)

Green Century Balanced (GCBLX)

Green Century Equity (GCEQX)

Guinness Atkinson Alternative Energy (GAAEX)

Legg Mason Investment Counsel Social Awareness (SSIAX)

Market Vectors Environmental Services ETF (EVX)

Market Vectors Global Alternative Energy ETF (GEX)

Market Vectors Solar Energy ETF (KWT)

New Alternatives Fund (NALFX)

PFW Water ETF (PFWAX)

Parnassus Equity Income (PRBLX)

Parnassus Fixed Income (PRFIX)

Parnassus Fund (PARNX)

Parnassus Mid-Cap Fund (PARMX)

Parnassus Small-Cap Fund (PARSX)

Parnassus Workplace Fund (PARWX)

Pax World Balanced Fund (PAXWX)

Pax World Global Green Fund (PGRNX)

Pax World Growth Fund (PXWGX)

Pax World High Yield Bond Fund (PAXHX)

Pax World International Fund (PXINX)

Pax World Small Cap Fund (PXSCX)

Pax World Womens Equity Fund (PXWEX)

Portfolio 21 (PORTX)

PowerShares Cleantech Portfolio (ETF:PZD)

PowerShares Global Water Portfolio (ETF: PIO)

PowerShares Water Resource (ETF: PHO)

PowerShares WilderHill Clean Energy (ETF: PBW)

PowerShares WilderHill Progressive Energy (ETF: PUW)

Sentinel Sustainable Core Opportunities (MYPVX)

Sentinel Sustainable Growth Opportunities (WAEGX)

Wells Fargo Advantage Social Sustainability Fund (WSSAX)

Winslow Green Growth (WGGFX)

Green Companies:

3PowerEnergy (**www.3powerenergy.com**): The 3Power Energy Group is a sustainable energy producer focused on global wind, solar, and hydro solutions. 3Power plans to provide its clients with green power on a utility scale.

Acciona (**www.acciona.com**): Acciona is a highly ranked wind farm developer but is active in all areas of clean energy.

Alstom (**www.alstom.com**): Alstom, a leader in transport infrastructure, power generation and transmission, has solutions for all energy sources (coal, gas, nuclear, fuel-oil, hydropower, wind) and is a leader in innovative technologies for the protection of the environment (reduction of CO_2 emissions, elimination of pollutant emissions).

Altaeros Energies (**www.altaerosenergies.com**): Altaeros Energies is developing an airborne wind turbine to produce renewable energy. Altaeros uses aerospace technology to lift wind turbines to higher heights.

Ampyx Power (**www.ampyxpower.com**): Ampyx is developing the PowerPlane, a device that can extract energy from the wind. The PowerPlane system consists of a sailplane flying patterns in the sky connected to a generator on the ground through a tether.

Aqua Sciences, Inc. (**www.aquasciences.com**): Aqua Sciences, Inc., was established to develop water technologies, including proprietary atmospheric water capture and purifications systems. Aqua Sciences' technology extracts water from the atmosphere virtually anywhere humans live.

Aquamarine Power (**www.aquamarinepower.com**): Aquamarine Power is the creator of the oyster wave energy technology.

Archer Daniels Midland (**www.adm.com**): Archer Daniels Midland Company turn crops into renewable products. They convert corn, oilseeds, wheat, and cocoa into products for food, animal feed, chemical, and energy uses.

AWS Ocean Energy (**www.awsocean.com**): AWS Ocean Energy develops the technology of choice for utility-scale generation of offshore wave power. They are the creator of the AWS-III: a multicell array of flexible membrane absorbers that covert wave power to pneumatic power through compression of air within each cell.

Beacon Power (**www.beaconpower.com**): Beacon Power designs and develops advanced products and services to support stable, reliable, and efficient electricity grid operation.

Broadwind Energy (**www.bwen.com**): Broadwind Energy creates gears and gearing systems for wind, oil, gas, and mining applications to wind towers, comprehensive remanufacturing of gearboxes and blades, operations and maintenance services, and specialty weldments.

Calpine (**www.calpine.com**): Calpine's fleet of natural-gas-fired plants are capable of delivering approximately 28,000 megawatts of clean, reliable electricity to customers and communities in 20 U.S. states and Canada.

Canadian Solar: (**www.canadiansolar.com**): Canadian Solar is one of the world's largest solar panel producers.

Centrotherm Photovoltaics (**www.centrotherm-pv.com**): Centrotherm Photovoltaics has three distinct product specialities: silicon and wafer, solar cell and module (including semiconductors and microelectronics) and thin-film module.

Citizenre (**www.citizenre.com**): The Citizenre Corporation is a solar energy developer of residential photovoltaic (PV) systems. They allow solar leasing of their products to homeowners for solar power generation.

City Windmills, Ltd. (**www.citywindmills.com**): City Windmills is a publicly traded company with headquarters in the United Kingdom and operating out of Geneva, Switzerland. They design small wind turbine systems.

Climate Change Capital (**www.climatechangecapital.com**): Climate Change Capital advises and invests in companies that recognize combating global warming is both a necessity and an economic opportunity.

Clean Wind Energy Tower, Inc. (**www.cleanwindenergytower.com**): Clean Wind Energy, Inc., is designing and preparing to develop and construct large "Downdraft Towers" that use benevolent, nontoxic natural elements to generate electricity and clean water.

Deeya Energy (**www.deeyaenergy.com**): Deeya Energy has engineered an energy storage platform. Their patented flow-battery technology offers superfast charging, large storage capacity, and high cycle life for five years operation.

Digi (**www.digi.com**): iDigi Energy is a solution bundle specifically for Energy Service Providers. iDigi Energy simplifies and accelerates the integration of energy management systems with remote energy assets.

DuPont (**www.dupont.com**): DuPont offers a wide range of products and services for markets including agriculture, nutrition, electronics, communications, safety and protection, home and construction, transportation, and apparel.

ECOtality, Inc. (**www.ecotality.com**): ECOtality is a leader in clean electric transportation and storage technologies.

Elster Solutions (**www.elstersolutions.com**): Elster Solutions specializes in electricity metering products and smart metering and smart-grid system solutions.

EnerVault (**www.enervault.com**): Enervault, a maker of flow-battery technology, offers solutions for grid-scale energy storage.

EVCARCO (**www.evcarco.com**): EV Car Company dedicated to bringing electric cars, hybrids, CNG, and alternative fuel vehicles to market.

Hain Celestial Group (**www.hain-celestial.com**): The Hain Celestial Group is a natural and organic food and personal care products company in North America and Europe.

Helion Energy (**www.helionenergy.com**): Helion Energy is in the process of harnessing fusion energy. They created the fusion engine, a technology for near-term fusion-based electricity generation.

Hemlock Semiconductor (**www.hscpoly.com**): Hemlock Semiconductor Group provides solar energy in the form of polycrystalline silicon semiconductors and photovoltaics.

Hitachi Transportation Systems (**www.hitachi-rail.com**): Hitachi Transportation Systems is one of the leading railway system suppliers.

Hyflux (**www.hyflux.com**): Hyflux is a leading provider of integrated water management and environmental solutions, especially desalination and water recycling efforts.

Iberdrola (**www.iberdrolarenewables.us**): Iberdrola Renewables, Inc., is the second-largest wind operator in the U.S. and operates natural gas storage.

Imperium Renewables (**www.imperiumrenewables.com**): Imperium Renewables produces biodiesel and continues to develop new biofuels.

JA Solar (**www.jasolar.com**): JA Solar's factories use advanced solar cell manufacturing equipment. The company has two main solar cell manufacturing facilities, one located in Ningjin, Hebei Province, and the other in Yangzhou, Jiangsu Province.

Joby Energy (**www.jobyenergy.com**): Joby Energy, Inc., is developing airborne wind turbines to harness the immense and consistent power in high-altitude wind.

Kona Blue Water Farms (**www.kona-blue.com**): Kona Blue Water Farms is the producer of the Kona Kampachi˚, a Hawaiian yellowtail that is open-ocean grown in the pristine waters off the Kona Coast of the

Big Island — hatched, reared and harvested using state-of-the-art aquaculture technology.

Konarka (**www.konarka.com**): Konarka concentrates on developing and producing solar technology to meet energy needs.

Magenn Power (**www.magenn.com**): Magenn Power researches and produces products that harness wind energy at high altitudes.

Makani Power (**www.makanipower.com**): Makani Power is developing airborne wind turbines (AWT) to extract energy from powerful, consistent winds at altitude.

Manz AG (**www.manz.com**): Manz in Reutlingen, Germany, has developed from an automation specialist to a provider of integrated system solutions for the production of crystalline silicon solar cells and thin-film solar modules, as well as the manufacturing of flat panel displays.

McCarthy (**www.mccarthy.com**): McCarthy is a construction company that specializes in green construction practices.

Monsanto (**www.monsanto.com**): Monsanto is an agricultural and vegetable seed producer that also develops genetically modified seeds and researches plant biotechnology traits.

Nanosolar (**www.nanosolar.com**): Applying the latest in robotic manufacturing — primarily from the automotive industry — Nanosolar assembles solar cells into solar panels and develops solar-powered film semiconductors.

Nanosys (**www.nanosysinc.com**): Nanosys is the creator of the quantum dot technology that works with DED-driven LCD backlight units. They also are working in collaboration with the world's leading lithium-ion battery manufacturers to deliver energy performance in new products using a new way of harnessing silicon for use in litherium-ion batteries.

North American Industries (**www.naicranes.com**): North American Industries designs complex monorail systems including curved tracks, multiple switches and interlocks, which permit monorails to interface with other material handling systems.

Oceanlinx Ltd (**www.oceanlinx.com**): Oceanlinx, a wave-energy developer in Australia, has installed more than 750KW of prototype plants, generating more than 40,000 hours of operating experience and 5,000 hours of electricity generation.

OceanSpar (**www.oceanspar.com**): OceanSpar develops products for marine aquaculture, including open ocean fish pens and mooring solutions.

OFT (**www.oceanfarmtech.com**): Ocean Farm Technologies Inc. develops and markets innovative technology for aquaculture in exposed open ocean conditions. They created the aquapod, a unique containment system for marine aquaculture, suited for rough open-ocean conditions and a diversity of species.

Ormat Technologies, Inc. (**www.ormat.com**): Ormat Technologies, Inc. develops solutions for geothermal power, recovered energy generation (REG), and remote power.

Power Tube, Inc. (**www.powertubeinc.com**): Power Tube, Inc., has developed the Geomagmatic Argus A-1 Power Tube, a new technology that uses geothermal energy, or the heat of the earth, to create energy.

Premier Power Renewable Energy, Inc. (**www.premierpower.com**): Premier Power is a leading solar power company providing solar panel systems for commercial, agricultural, industrial, government, utility, and residential customers.

Prudent Energy (**www.pdenergy.com**): Prudent Energy, a clean energy company, is the designer, manufacturer, and integrator of the patented vanadium redox battery energy storage system (VRB-ESS˚) — a large-capacity energy storage system.

RavenBrick (**www.ravenbrick.com**): RavenBrick concentrates on producing smart-window technology designed to cut down on energy use. RavenWindow™ is the company's signature product.

Renewable Energy Corporation (REC) (**www.recgroup.com/en/recgroup**): Renewable Energy Corporation is a player in the solar energy industry. REC is among the world's largest producers of polysilicon and wafers for solar applications and a rapidly growing manufacturer of solar cells and modules.

RentalSolar.com (**www.rentalsolar.com**): RentalSolar.com is a Web-based company that allows customers to rent solar equipment with all expenses paid for by the manufacturer. The customer pays for the energy produced.

RentSolar.com (**www.rentsolar.com**): RentSolar.com is a Web-based company that allows customers to rent solar equipment. They pay by the month, and the solar energy powers their houses.

Siemens (**www.siemens.com**): Siemens' Energy Sector is a leading supplier of a wide range of products, solutions and services for power generation, transmission, and distribution as well as for the production. Their energy-efficient products and solutions also are contributing to environmental protection.

Sky WindPower (**www.skywindpower.com**): Sky WindPower's flying electric generators are meant to capture the energy of high-altitude winds.

Soladigm (**www.soladigm.com**): Soladigm is a developer of green building solutions designed to improve energy efficiency. The company's dynamic glass switches from clear to tinted on demand.

Southwest Windpower (**www.windenergy.com**): Southwest Windpower creates battery-powered wind turbines for commercial and residential use.

Spectra (**www.spectrawatermakers.com**): Spectra Watermakers Inc. is a well-respected marine equipment distributor and systems engineering firm. Their reverse osmosis desalinization system, the Spectra Watermachine, requires only 13 watt-hours per gallon, just 33 percent of the energy required by the best competitive technology.

Syngenta (**www.syngenta.com**): Syngenta is an agriculture producer that develops seeds and plants resistant to plant diseases and infestations.

Tesla (**www.teslamotors.com**): Tesla designs and manufactures EVs and EV power-train components. They designed the Roadster, the first electronic sports car.

Tokuyama Corporation (**www.tokuyama.co.jp/eng/index.html**): The Tokuyama Corporation incorporates a broad array of businesses ranging from organic and inorganic chemicals to plastics, cement/building materials, and electronics materials.

Trina Solar (**www.trinasolar.com**): Trina Solar's modules provide clean and reliable solar electric power in on-grid and off-grid residential, commercial, industrial, and utility-scale systems

Turner Construction (**www.turnerconstruction.com**): Turner is the largest builder of green buildings in the nation and has experience across a wide variety of sustainable construction projects.

United Natural Foods (**www.unfi.com**): UNFI is an independent national distributor of natural, organic, and specialty foods and related products, including nutritional supplements, personal care items, and organic produce.

United Technologies Corporation (UTC) (**www.utc.com**): United Technologies is a diversified company whose products include Carrier heating and air conditioning, Hamilton Sundstrand aerospace systems and industrial products, Otis elevators and escalators, Pratt & Whitney aircraft engines, Sikorsky helicopters, UTC fire and security systems, and UTC power fuel cells.

UQM Technologies (**www.uqm.com**): UQM Technologies is a developer and manufacturer of power-dense, high-efficiency electric motors, generators, and power electronic controllers.

Vestas (**www.vestas.com**): Vestas is a leader in wind technology, with a history of technological innovation and more than 30 years of experience in developing, manufacturing, installing, and maintaining wind turbines.

Wacker Chemie AG (**www.wacker.com/cms/en/home/index.jsp**): Wacker is one of the largest silicone manufacturers of silicone fluids, emulsions, resins, elastomers, and sealants to silanes and pyrogenic silicas.

Appendix B: Resources

Websites

Eco Stocks (**www.ecostocks.com**): Eco Stocks provides industry news, stock profiles, and blogs for members.

Database of State Incentives for Renewables and Efficiency website (**www. dsireusa.org**): A database and directory of government tax deductions for using or installing green equipment

Green Chip Stocks (**www.greenchipstocks.com**): Green Chip Stocks has news about the green investing industry.

Green Stock Exchange (**http://greensx.com**): Opening in fall 2012, Green Stock Exchange will be an international electronic bulletin board for direct trading of shares in social businesses.

Green Stocks Rock.com (**www.greenstocksrock.com**): Green Stocks Rock. com provides industry news for all the green options and gives viewers videos on green choices in the stock world.

GreenStocks Central (**http://greenstockscentral.com**): GreenStocks Central provides information about many green companies as well as discussion boards for members and information on each of the green industries.

Investor Ideas (**www.investorideas.com**): An overall resource for news about the green industries, Investor Ideas also offers directories of green stock options for sale.

Speculating Green (**www.speculatinggreen.com**): Speculating Green has green stock and trading advice, as well as industry news and newsletters.

Sustainable Business.com (**www.sustainablebusiness.com**): Sustainable Business.com lists stocks and their rankings and is sortable by industry. It also has links to advice for green investing and a job listing of green jobs.

Additional Reading:

Matthew J. Kiernan. *Investing in a Sustainable World*. AMACOM, 2009.

Ron Pernick and Clint Wilder, *The Clean-tech Revolution*. Harper, 2008.

John Rubino. *Clean Money*. John Wiley & Sons, Inc., 2009.

Jack Uldrich. *Green Investing*. Adams Media, 2010.

Glossary of Terms

Afforestation: Planting trees, typically to generate carbon offsets to allow more carbon dioxide emission from a plant or process

Alpha: The measure of performance of a fund over and above a benchmark, taking account of the volatility. For example, if a fund with a certain volatility or risk should make 10 percent, but the subject fund makes 15 percent, the alpha would be 5 percent, the excess over the benchmark.

Alternative energy: Energy from something other than the recognized main sources, such as coal, oil, natural gas, nuclear, etc.

American Stock Exchange (AMEX): A stock exchange that used to specialize in small-cap stocks and has now merged with the NASDAQ

Ask price: The price at which a security is offered for sale, sometimes called the offer

Asset allocation: Investing with a carefully calculated mix of assets to reduce portfolio risk, increase portfolio return, or a combination of the two

Automatic reinvestment: A system to reinvest dividends or other earnings into the security, buying additional shares

Back-end load: The fee charged by some funds on selling the fund shares

Balance sheet: Summary of the company's financial position, including assets, liabilities, and shareholders' equity

Bankruptcy: Inability of a person or company to pay its debts

Basis point: Equal to one 100th of one percent and used to denote the change in a financial instrument

Bear market: A market where prices are going down

Below par: The price less than the face value of a security

Benchmark: A standard used to judge a fund manager's performance

Beta: A measure of risk in financial instruments

Bid price: The price the buyer is willing to pay for a security

Biodegradable: Substances that will break down and be reabsorbed into the ecosystem

Biodiesel: Diesel fuel made from organic material, whether from waste oil or from crops grown for the purpose

Bioenergy: Any form of energy that comes from biological matter, which includes from crops, trees, or even algae

Biofuels: Fuels that are made from recent organic material, as opposed to those from fossil sources; includes biodiesel and ethanol made from corn

Blue chip stocks: Common stocks of large well-known companies that have a history of good growth and dividends

Bonds: Financial instruments of debt

Bond fund: A fund that invests in bonds

Book value: The value of the company's assets, minus any liabilities

Broker: An individual or company that deals in the funds or other securities for the public

Bull market: A market where prices are rising in an uptrend

Cap and trade: A trading system pioneered in the U.S. in the 1980s that places a limit or "cap" on the amount of emissions permitted. Trading of emissions is allowed between the participants, which means money can be realized for reducing emissions substantially, or alternatively, emissions can be maintained at a cost. Over time, the permitted amount of emission is reduced.

Capital gains or losses: The difference between the selling price of an asset and the price originally paid

Capital gains distributions: These are payments to mutual fund shareholders of gains that the fund has realized in the year from sales at a profit, less any losses.

Carbon dioxide: A naturally occurring gas, a product of breathing and of normal combustion; when emitted in excess, considered to be one of the gases responsible for climate change

Carbon dioxide equivalent: The scale used for measuring the effect of greenhouse gases. It expresses the effects of other greenhouse gases, such as methane, in terms of the equivalent amount of carbon dioxide.

Carbon footprint: The amount of carbon dioxide produced by human activities. This can be measured on a personal basis or refer to companies or society as a whole.

Carbon neutral: A process that does not produce carbon dioxide emissions or that has those emissions offset elsewhere

Carbon offset: A reduction in greenhouse gas emissions, expressed in terms of quantity of carbon dioxide

Carbon sequestration: Process of removing carbon dioxide from the atmosphere, which may be by natural means growing more plants and trees or by physically extracting it and storing it underground

CFL: Stands for compact fluorescent light, a type of light bulb, which replaces a standard bulb, is much more energy efficient, and has a longer life.

Climate change: A sometimes controversial idea that there is a change in weather patterns resulting from an increase in greenhouse gases; previously called global warming, but this term has fallen into disuse as some weather changes result in colder conditions, giving critics an opportunity to ridicule the idea.

Close a position: To end a trade, usually by selling all the shares in a long position, or by "buying to cover" a short position

Closed-end fund: A mutual fund with a fixed number of shares, usually listed on a stock exchange

Commodities: Large amounts of unprocessed goods, such as grains and metals, traded on the exchange

Concentrated solar power: A system to track the sun with mirrors that reflect the sun's light onto a small area.

Contrarian: The trader who goes against the market

Correction: When a security dips in value temporarily from people taking profits

Cost basis: The original cost of an investment

Coupon: The interest rate paid on the bond until maturity

Currency risk: In a global investing, the chance that currency exchange rates will vary to the detriment of the investor

Depression: A long-term decline in the economy

Derivative: A type of investment whose value is derived from an underlying security

Discount broker: A brokerage firm that executes orders at a low rate of commission

Discount rate: The interest rate that the Federal Reserve charges a bank to borrow funds

Diversification: Investing in different market sectors to avoid any particular market weakness affecting the whole portfolio

Dividend: May be paid to stockholders from company profits

Dividend reinvestment plan: Also shortened to DRIP, a system to automatically reinvest any dividends paid back into the security, buying more shares

Dollar cost averaging: The system of investing in securities with a regular fixed payment, which averages the price paid

Earnings: The net income of a company

Earnings per share: Total earnings for the company divided by the number of shares outstanding

Earth Day: An annual global event that celebrates nature and the environment; takes place on April 22.

EBIDTA: Company earnings before interest, debt, taxes, and amortization

Eco-friendly: A term casually used to describe services or products that are deemed less harmful to the environment than standard items; typically used as a "buzzword."

Electric cars: Vehicles that run solely by using an electric motor

Emerging-market fund: A fund that invests in a growing market

Emission reduction: Any system that removes or lessens the emission of greenhouse gases

Energy audit: A way to determine how much and in which way energy is being used in a building, so managers can devise ways to save the energy consumption.

Energy conservation: Reducing the amount of energy used

Energy consumption: The amount of energy used, typically applied to appliances to give comparative ratings of efficiency

Environmental awareness: Recognition of environmental issues when making choices

Equity: A stock, or the value of securities in a brokerage account

Ethanol: Also known as ethyl alcohol, which is found in alcoholic beverages as well; can be manufactured from common materials, such as corn, sugar cane, and even plant waste.

Exchange-traded fund (ETF): The fund, usually a simple index fund, which trades on an exchange. Unlike a mutual fund, the value is not fixed by the holdings but varies with supply and demand on the exchange.

Expense ratio: The percentage of the funds assets used to meet expenses, such as management and office fees

FDIC: The Federal Deposit Insurance Corporation, which promotes confidence in banks by insuring deposits against bank failure

Federal Reserve Board: An agency responsible for setting fiscal policy by regulating the discount rate

Fee-only adviser: A financial adviser who charges a set rate, rather than receiving income from commission on products traded

Fixed income: Income from a financial instrument paying a fixed rate, such as bonds

Fossil fuel: Fuels such as gas, oil, and coal, which were formed over millions of years from decaying plant and animal life

Front-end load: A sales fee charged at the time of buying some funds — cf back-end load

Fuel cell: A chemical device that produces electricity. Often seen as a hydrogen fuel cell, which combines hydrogen with oxygen from the atmosphere, forming water as it creates power; different from a battery, in that the chemical is replenished to recharge the cell.

Fuel consumption: Amount of fuel used by a vehicle, typically measured as miles per gallon in the U.S., or liters per 100 kilometers in European countries

Fuel economy, fuel efficiency: Similar to fuel consumption, but with a greater emphasis on how little fuel is used

Fund: Organized by a financial company, an investment organization in which you can invest in shares or other financial instruments

Fund of funds: A fund that invests in other mutual funds

Fundamental analysis: Examining the true worth of a company, in terms of its assets, sales, expenses, etc., in order to assess the long-term value of the shares

Gas mileage: Another term for fuel consumption

Geothermal heat pump: A heating and cooling system that uses fluid circulated underground as a heat sink, which is typically very efficient

Global fund: A mutual fund that invests in shares from around the world

Global warming: A term previously used for climate change

Green buildings: Energy efficient and sustainable buildings, usually better than conventionally constructed buildings

Green energy: Energy produced from renewable resources, such as solar and wind power

Green products: A term loosely used to describe products that are better for the environment

Greenhouse gases: Gases in the atmosphere that trap heat from escaping the Earth. They occur naturally and include water vapor and carbon dioxide. Without them, the Earth would be colder. The increase in human activity and emissions of greenhouse gases has been blamed for climate change. To explore your personal contribution, you can find a greenhouse gas emission calculator on the EPA website, at **www.epa. gov/climatechange/emissions/ ind_calculator.html**.

Gross Domestic Product (GDP): The output of the nation generated within the country's boundaries

Growth fund: A fund that specifically seeks capital gain in choosing investments

Hedge: A financial strategy to offset potential losses in one security against another

Hedge fund: An investment fund that is able to use many strategies, including derivatives and shortselling, to optimize returns

Hybrid cars: Vehicles such as the Toyota Prius that use more than one fuel. It uses stored electricity as well as a conventional gasoline engine.

Hydroelectric energy: Electricity resulting from the flow of water, typically by using a dam to hold back water reserves, which allows a controlled flow through turbine generators

Hydrogen engine: An internal combustion engine that runs on hydrogen rather than gasoline or diesel fuel

Index: A measure of the value of shares in a market, such as the Dow Jones Industrial Average, the S&P 500, the NASDAQ, the FTSE 100, etc.

Index fund: A mutual fund or exchange-traded funds designed to mimic the value of a stock market index

Inflation risk: The risk that inflation will reduce or make negative the returns on a particular investment

Interest rate risk: The risk that the value of a bond will decline because of a rise in general interest rates

International fund: A mutual fund that invests in shares from outside the United States

Investment adviser: A person qualified by experience and examination to assist in investment decisions

Investment Advisers Act: A law passed in 1940 that governs the actions of investment advisers

Junk bonds: A bond with a low credit rating and a compensatory high yield for those prepared to take the risk

Kyoto Protocol: An agreement negotiated in 1997 in Kyoto, Japan, that gives industrialized nations emissions targets; not ratified by the U.S.

Large cap: One of the companies with the largest capitalization

Leverage: Applied to investing, leverage involves increasing the power of your investment, usually by investing only part of the cost and using some form of borrowing for the remainder

LED lighting: An alternative to the CFL, an energy efficient and long-lasting type of light bulb

LEED: Leadership in Energy and Environmental Design, a program for certification of the design, construction, and operation of green buildings

Life-cycle fund: A fund in which investments are changed over time to suit an anticipated date for redemption

Liquidate: Converting assets into cash

Liquidity: A measure of how quickly a security can be sold for a fair price

Load: A sales charge

Load fund: A mutual fund that has a sales charge

Long: Holding financial securities in order to profit if the price increases

Long-Term Equity Anticipation Securities (LEAPS): Publicly traded options contracts that have an expiration longer than one year

Low-load fund: A mutual fund that charges 3 ½ percent or less as its load

Management fee: The amount paid to the investment adviser

Market capitalization: The value of the company; the share price times the number of shares outstanding

Master fund: A fund that invests in other funds

Maturity: The date when the principal is to be paid back on a bond

Mid cap: A large company, but smaller than the large-cap companies. Different markets set different levels of capitalization.

Money market: Lending or borrowing funds for less than three years

Money-market fund: A fund that invests in short-term securities

Municipal bond: A government-issued bond

Mutual fund: An investment fund operated by a company

National Association of Security Dealers (NASD): A self-regulatory organization of the securities industry responsible for the operation and regulation of the NASDAQ stock market and over-the-counter markets; also administrated exams for investment professionals, such as the Series 7 exam

Net asset value (NAV): The value of a mutual fund holding, calculated from the securities held less liabilities, divided by the number of fund shares outstanding

Net worth: The total value of all assets and possessions minus the total of liabilities and debts

No-load fund: A mutual fund that has no sales charges or commissions

Nominal return: The way most returns are quoted. The nominal return does not make allowance for inflation.

New York Stock Exchange (NYSE): A stock exchange located in lower Manhattan, New York City, is the world's largest stock exchange.

Off-the-grid: Term usually applied to electricity, it refers to a building or dwelling that has no external utility connection, but is arranged to be self-sufficient.

On-demand water heater: Sometimes called an instant water heater, this heats water only when needed

and does not have a storage reservoir.

Open-end fund: A fund without limitation on issuing or redeeming shares

Operating expenses: The costs associated with running a fund, which include management fees and expenses

Options: Associated more with short-term trading than investing, options are a form of lining up potential trades without committing to them. You can buy the right to make the trade at some time in the future but are not forced to if there would be no profit or a loss for you.

Over-the-counter (OTC): This means that the stock is traded in some other way than on a formal exchange.

Paper loss: A loss in a security that has yet to be sold

Par: The face value of a security

Peak oil: A time when the maximum rate of production of

oil globally has been reached and from which output will decline in successive years. Some observers claim that this time already has been reached.

Photovoltaic: A method of converting sunlight directly into electricity, usually accomplished at this time with solar panels

Portfolio: A collection of equities, bonds, and other financial instruments held by an individual or by a company

Premium: Amount by which the price of the security exceeds the face value

Price-to-earnings ratio (P/E): The stock price divided by the per-share earnings for the last year; commonly used as a guide to whether a stock is overvalued or undervalued

Price-to-sales ratio (P/S): The stock price divided by the sales per share for the last year

Prospectus: A document that describes the investment, such as a mutual fund, to potential shareholders

Real estate investment trust (REIT): The company that manages a group of real estate investments and in which you can buy shares

Real return: The real return is the return after adjustment for inflation

Rebalancing: The process of restoring the target allocations of different types of securities in your portfolio

Recession: A downturn in the economy that is defined as a drop in Gross National Product for two successive quarters

Recycle: To reuse an otherwise waste item. Many communities now recycle glass, aluminum, steel, cardboard, and other things.

Renewable resources: Natural resources which continually regenerate, such as solar and wind power.

Renewable energy: Electricity produced from renewable resources such as wind and solar

REITs: Real estate investment trusts; companies that earn income from rental or mortgages of properties

Return on assets (ROA): The company's net earnings divided by its total assets; usually expressed as a percentage

Return on equity (ROE): The company's net earnings divided by its equity expressed as a percentage and indicating how well a company is managing its resources

Return on investment (ROI): A measure of the efficiency of investment, which can be used to compare different investments; the return on the investment divided by the cost expressed as a percentage

Risk tolerance: An investor's willingness to tolerate the ups and downs of a security's price

ROI: Return on investment, or income divided by the investment

Sales charge: Otherwise known as load; a charge to investors for buying or redeeming their shares in a fund

Sector fund: A mutual fund that specializes in investing in a particular market sector

Securities and Exchange Commission (SEC): The government agency that regulates much of investment, including the markets, funds, financial advisers, and brokers

Shares: Ownership in a company

Shareholders: Shareholders buy shares in a company and own (a part of) the company; they can vote, at least annually, on company policies and appoint the board of directors.

Small cap: Companies that are less capitalized than mid cap

Solar energy: Energy created from the sun, which may either be electricity or by direct heating

Solar power: Electricity created from the sun

Solar water heating: Hot water created directly from the sun's power

Standard & Poor's (S&P): A company that rates stocks, bonds, and credit and issues indices of values

Standard deviation: Standard deviation is a measure of investment volatility, or how much it varies over time

Stock: Ownership of part of a company

Stop-loss order: An order to your broker to sell a stock if it falls to a certain price level

Sustainability: Development meeting the needs of the present without compromising the ability of future generations to meet their own needs

Tax-exempt bond: Usually issued by a municipality or government agency, a bond which has tax advantages on the gains

Tax-free fund: A fund that makes investments that are not taxable

Total return: The total return is the combination of growth in value and the income or dividend

Treasury bill: U.S. debt obligation with a maturity date less than one year

Treasury bond: U.S. debt obligation with a maturity date of ten or more years

Treasury note: U.S. debt obligation with a maturity date from one year to ten years

Trend: The direction of the market

Volatility: The amount of fluctuation in the price of a security; sometimes expressed mathematically as for example "standard deviation"

Wall Street: The physical home of the NYSE and many financial companies

Wind energy: Energy created from the wind's power; usually refers to electricity

Wind farms: Groups of wind turbines located adjacent to each other

Wind turbines: Machines that generate electricity from the force of the wind

Author Biography

Alan Northcott is a successful financial author, freelance writer, trading educator, professional engineer, radio broadcaster, farmer, karaoke jockey, and wedding officiant, along with other pursuits. He and his wife are moving from Colorado to Florida, and they share their houses with many dogs and cats. They have three children living on three different continents and two grandchildren.

Originating from England, Northcott was educated at Eltham College in London and obtained his degree from the University of Surrey, in England. He immigrated with his wife to America in 1992. His engineering career spanned more than 30 years on both sides of the Atlantic. Recent years have found him seeking and living a more diverse, fulfilling lifestyle. This is the ninth financial book he has written, all which are available from At-lantic Publishing Group, Inc.

He offers a free newsletter on various related and unrelated topics. You can e-mail him directly at **alannorthcott@msn.com** for more details.

Index